Interpreting European Financial Statements

Interpreting European Financial Statements

Christopher Nobes
Coopers & Lybrand Professor of Accounting
University of Reading

Second Edition

Butterworths
London, Dublin and Edinburgh
1994

United Kingdom	Butterworth & Co (Publishers) Ltd, 88 Kingsway, LONDON WC2B 6AB and 4 Hill Street, EDINBURGH EH2 3JZ
Australia	Butterworths Pty Ltd, SYDNEY, MELBOURNE, BRISBANE, ADELAIDE, PERTH, CANBERRA and HOBART
Belgium	Butterworth & Co (Publishers) Ltd, BRUSSELS
Canada	Butterworth Canada Ltd, TORONTO and VANCOUVER
Ireland	Butterworth (Ireland) Ltd, DUBLIN
Malaysia	Malayan Law Journal Sdn Bhd, KUALA LUMPUR
New Zealand	Butterworths of New Zealand Ltd, WELLINGTON and AUCKLAND
Puerto Rico	Butterworths of Puerto Rico Inc, SAN JUAN
Singapore	Malayan Law Journal Pte Ltd, SINGAPORE
USA	Butterworth Legal Publishers, CARLSBAD, California, and SALEM, New Hampshire

First edition 1989

A CIP Catalogue record for this book is available from the British Library.

ISBN 0 406 02882 6

Typeset by Latimer Trend & Co Ltd, Plymouth
Printed and bound in Great Britain by Mackays of Chatham PLC,
Chatham, Kent.

to

Michael, Mona and Sidney

Preface

Since the first edition of the book (called *Interpreting European Financial Statements: Towards 1992*) several important changes have occurred:

- the title has passed its date mark;
- Eastern European countries have begun to revolutionise their accounting systems;
- the EC accounting Directives have been implemented in all EC countries;
- several non-EC countries have applied to join the EC and have already approximated their accounting laws;
- the EC Commission has decided to issue no further accounting Directives, but has embarked on other ways of pursuing harmonisation.

This second edition takes account of these changes, and makes numerous other minor up-datings.

Christopher Nobes
University of Reading
January 1994

Preface to the First Edition

This book is a companion volume to *Interpreting US Financial Statements* by the same author and publisher. To some extent the structure of the two books is similar, particularly in the subject matter of Chapter 1 and in the order of material in Chapters 5 to 8. However, UK and US accounting can be seen as belonging to the same family; whereas accounting practices within Europe differ greatly. These differences are a major commercial problem, particularly for a unifying market such as the European Communities. The words 'Towards 1992' in this book's title correctly suggest the emphasis given in several parts of this book to the harmonisation process in the EC.

This book is intended primarily for such users as financial managers and auditors of multinationals and for international analysts, investors and lenders. References are kept to a minimum, given the book's largely practical rather than academic purpose. The book is designed to be useful to readers in any country, both within and without the EC. Where one European country is needed as a basis for comparison, the benchmark tends to be the UK, which is the home country of the largest number of listed companies in Europe. This benchmark will also make the book as accessible as possible to readers in North America, Australasia and the East.

In preparing this book, I have been greatly assisted by Bob Parker of Exeter University, who has made many comments on previous drafts.

The world of European accounting changes very fast, and particularly in the late 1980s and the 1990s. This book is designed to be up-to-date in late 1989, but some of its details will be overtaken by subsequent events.

Christopher Nobes
University of Reading
September 1989

Contents

CHAPTER 1

The Background to European Accounting

1.1 Introduction

The Europeanness of Accounting

Double-entry bookkeeping, listed companies, accountancy professions and published financial statements are all European inventions. The exact geography of inventions seems to be driven by commerce. For example, the increasing complexity of business in late Medieval northern Italy led to the emergence of double entry; the existence of a wealthy merchant class and the need for large investment for major projects led to public subscription of share capital in seventeenth-century Holland; the growing separation of ownership from management raised the need for audit in nineteenth-century Britain. Many countries have contributed: France led in the development of the profit and loss account; Germany gave us standardised formats for financial statements.

The Structure of the Book

The diversity of these European origins is reflected in the present differences in reporting practices in Europe. The continent is rich in the variety of its legal systems, commercial practices and ownership structures. This also contributes to the differences in accounting. A study of the background will illuminate the practical problems: and that is the subject of this first chapter.

It is increasingly the case that European companies and individuals are investing in or lending to companies in other European countries. For Britain the trend away from the Commonwealth and the USA and towards Europe has been visible since the Second World War. This trend has accelerated dramatically since entry to the European Communities (EC)[1] and particularly since the unified market of 1992 onwards. This means that European accounting differences have become increasingly noticeable and damaging. They militate against cross-border investment and, within multinational companies, they hamper the appraisal of performance, the work of

[1] In November 1993, the EC became part of a wide arrangement of organisations called the European Union. This book retains the usage 'EC'.

auditors and the movement of staff. The broad categories of difference are examined in Chapter 2.

Because of the bewildering mass of differences and the large number of countries that one could be interested in, it is useful to try to perceive a pattern in Europe. That is, it may be possible to put countries into groups by the similarity of their reporting practices. This is attempted in Chapter 3. A classification of countries can be used to impose some order on apparent chaos and to speed up the learning process: knowledge of one country can be used to draw inferences about others.

Having examined the causes and nature of differences, it is then appropriate to look at harmonisation of accounting within the EC. This has been in progress since the 1970s, but there is still a long way to go. The basic mechanism for achieving harmonisation is change to company laws in the member states, driven by Directives which are drafted by the Commission and adopted by the Council of Ministers. These matters are the subject of Chapter 4.

The detailed differences in practice, still remaining after the harmonisation of the 1980s, are examined in Chapters 5 to 8 which deal, respectively, with presentation of accounts, asset valuation, profit measurement and group accounting. These differences are summarised in Chapter 9 which goes on to propose an international benchmark for comparison of European financial statements. Of course, language differences are also a problem, and these are addressed in a glossary at the end of the book.

There are many countries in Europe. This book will be confined to the highly developed countries of Western Europe. Furthermore, as has been mentioned, there will be frequent reference to differences and harmonisation within the EC. Even within the EC, there are 12 countries in the middle of the 1990s, and it is impossible to deal with them all in detail. Illustrations tend to be drawn from major commercial countries such as France, Germany and the Netherlands. It is also the case that discussion is generally centred around the practices of large companies.

There is a note on Eastern Europe at the end of this chapter.

Causes of Difference

The rest of this chapter deals with the probable causes of European differences in financial reporting. A study of this will help to set the differences into context. It will enable the reader to appreciate that the present differences are deep-seated and long-lasting.

There seems to be some consensus about which factors are involved in shaping financial reporting. Some researchers have used impressions of such causes as a means of differentiating between countries (Mueller, 1967, Part II). Other researchers have studied whether perceived differences in accounting practices correlate with such perceived causal factors (Frank, 1979). Factors which are seen as influencing accounting development include the nature of the legal system, the prevalent providers of finance, the influence of taxation, and the strength of the accountancy profession.

On a world-wide scale, factors like language or geography have been referred to by the above-mentioned researchers. To the extent that these do have some explanatory power, it seems more sensible to assume that this results from auto-correlation. That is, the fact that Australian accounting bears a marked resemblance to New Zealand accounting might be 'confirmed' by language and geographical factors. However, most of their similarities were probably not *caused* by these factors, but by their historical connection with the UK which passed on both accounting and language, and was colonising most parts of Australasia in the same period.

Further, if one wanted to encompass countries outside the developed western world, it would be necessary to include factors concerning the state of development of the economy and the nature of the political economy of the countries concerned. Of course, to some extent a precise definition of terms might make it clear that it was impossible to include some such countries. For example, if our interest is in the financial reporting practices of listed corporations, those countries with few or no such corporations have to be excluded. Fortunately, as our main purpose concerns Western Europe, there is a reasonable degree of homogeneity, in that they all have developed economies, democratic governments, listed companies, qualified accountants, and so on. For our purposes, the following seven factors may cumulate to a powerful explanation of the cause of financial reporting differences: legal systems, providers of finance, taxation, the accountancy profession, inflation, theory, and accidents.

1.2 Legal Systems

Most European countries have a system of law which is based on the Roman *ius civile* as compiled by Justinian in the sixth century and developed by European universities from the twelfth century. Here rules are linked to ideas of justice and morality; they become doctrine. The word 'codified' may be associated with such a system. This has the important effect that company law or commercial codes need to establish rules in detail for accounting and financial reporting. For example, in the Netherlands, accounting law is contained in Book 2 of the Civil Code; in Germany and France, the Commercial Code contains accounting rules which are supplemented by company law and, in France, by a government-controlled 'accounting plan' (see Chapter 2).

On the other hand, the UK and Ireland have a commercial legal system which has relied upon a limited amount of statute law. This is because the environment has been the 'common law' system that was formed in England primarily by post-Conquest judges acting on the king's behalf. It is less abstract than codified law; a common law rule seeks to provide an answer to a specific case rather than to formulate a general rule for the future. Although this common law system emanates from England, it may be found in similar forms in many countries influenced by England. Thus, the federal law of the USA, the laws of India, Australia, and so on are to a greater or lesser extent modelled on English common law. This naturally influences company law, which traditionally does not prescribe a large number of detailed, all-embracing rules to cover the behaviour of companies and how they should publish their financial statements. To a large extent, accounting within such a context is not dependent upon law. This was certainly the case in the UK until the Companies Act 1981 introduced rules from an EC Directive (see Chapter 4). Until then, the only legal instruction on matters of accounting presentation or measurement was that the accounts should 'give a true and fair view'. Denmark has a similar legal tradition.

Table 1.1 Some European Legal Systems

Common Law	**Roman, Codified**
England and Wales	France
Ireland	Italy
	Germany
(United States)	Spain
(Canada)	Netherlands
(Australia)	
(New Zealand)	(Japan, commercial)

Note: the laws of Scotland, Israel, South Africa, Quebec, Louisiana and the Philippines embody elements of both systems.

Table 1.2 Some European Company Names

	Private	**Public**
France, Belgium, Luxembourg, Switzerland	Société à responsibilité limitée (Sàrl)	Société anonyme (SA)
Italy	Società a responsibilità limitata (SRL)	Società per Azioni (SpA)
Netherlands, Belgium	Besloten vennootschap (BV)	Naamloze vennootschap (NV)
Spain	Sociedad de responsibilidad limitada (SRL)	Sociedad anònima (SA)
UK, Ireland	Private limited company (Ltd)	Public limited company (PLC)
Germany, Switzerland	Gesellschaft mit beschränkter Haftung (GmbH)	Aktiengessellschaft (AG)
Denmark	Anpartsselskab (APS)	Aktieselskab (A/S)

This difference in legal traditions means that accounting rules tend to be law-based and slow to change in 'Roman' countries, whereas the detail is controlled by accountants in 'English' countries. This affects both the nature of regulation and the nature of the detailed rules in a country.

Table 1.1 above illustrates the way in which some European countries' legal systems divide between these two types (a few other countries are included for comparison).

It will be useful at this point to discuss the nature of companies. The great bulk of business in Europe is handled by limited companies, the most common forms of which are the public company and the private company. Table 1.2 above shows the names and abbreviations of these for some

European countries. The general distinction is that only for public companies is there allowed to be a market in their securities, such as a listing on a stock exchange.

Public companies are less numerous than private companies, and the laws relating to them are stricter. For example, public companies have more onerous requirements relating to minimum capital and to profit distribution. A further difference in 'Roman law' countries is that public companies tend to have bearer shares, as opposed to registered shares. This means that there is often no share register. Public companies may then be literally anonymous (*anonyme*) or nameless (*naamloze*).

In some countries, there is no legal distinction between the public and the private company. This is the case in Sweden, Norway and Finland, where limited companies are all of the joint-stock company form, like the German AG. The initials in these three Nordic countries are AB, AS and Oy, respectively. This lack of legal distinction between public and private companies is also the case in the USA (see Nobes, 1988).

1.3 Providers of Finance

The prevalent types of business organisation and ownership also differ. In France and Italy, capital provided by the state or by banks is very significant, as are small and large family businesses. In Germany, the banks in particular are important owners of companies as well as providers of debt finance. A majority of shares in some public companies is owned or controlled as proxies by banks, particularly by the Deutsche, Dresdner and Commerz Banks. The importance of banks is increased by the prevalence of bearer shares, as mentioned above. In Germany, for example, shareholders are required to deposit their valuable bearer share certificates with their bank, which then collects dividends and exercises proxy votes. As a result of this multi-faceted influence, banks are often represented on boards of directors.

By contrast, British companies tend to be funded by share finance and to have lower gearing. Furthermore, the share finance is very widely spread, particularly compared to continental Europe. The country with the longest history of 'public' companies is the Netherlands. Although it has a fairly small Stock Exchange, shares in many large companies are widely held and actively traded.

Evidence that this characterisation is reasonable may be found by looking at the number of listed companies in various countries. Table 1.3 overleaf shows the numbers of domestic listed shares on Stock Exchanges where there are over 500 such companies. The comparison between the UK and Germany or France is instructive. A two-group categorisation of these countries is almost as obvious as that for legal systems in Table 1.1 (taking account of size of economy and population).

Upon closer examination, the split between UK-type and continental-type is even starker. First, the continental European (and Japanese) numbers are misleadingly high because of the importance of 'insider' owners, non-voting and preference shares, and cross-holdings. Secondly, the UK/US numbers need to be added to by unlisted markets and over-the-counter stocks.

Although it is to some extent the case that shares in countries like the UK (and the USA) are held by institutional investors rather than by individual shareholders, this still contrasts with state, bank or family holdings. Indeed,

Table 1.3 Stock Exchanges with over 500 Domestic Listed Companies (and market value over £50 bn)

Exchange	Companies	Market value £ bn
Australia	968	77
Germany	665	210
Johannesburg	698	99
Korea	694	52
London	1,915	541
Montreal	589	129
NASDAQ (US)	3,841	292
New York	1,780	1,896
Paris	551	186
Tokyo	1,641	1,616
Toronto	1,069	143

Source: *Stock Exchange Quarterly*, London Stock Exchange, April–June 1992.

the increased importance of institutional investors is perhaps a reinforcement for the following hypothesis:

> In countries with a widespread ownership of companies by shareholders who do not have access to internal information there will be a pressure for disclosure, audit and 'fair' information.

Institutional investors hold larger blocks of shares and may be better organised than private shareholders; thus their desire for information and their command of resources should increase this pressure, although they may also be able successfully to press for more detailed information than is generally available to the public.

'Fair' was mentioned in the previous section and still needs to be defined. It is a concept related to those large number of outside owners who require unbiased information about the success of the business and its state of affairs (Stamp, 1980; Flint, 1982). Although reasonable prudence will be expected, these shareholders are interested in comparing one year with another and one company with another, thus the accruals concept and some degree of realism will be required. This entails judgment which entails experts. This expertise is also required for the checking of the financial statements by auditors. In countries like the UK and the Netherlands, over many decades this can result in a tendency to require accountants to work out their own technical rules. This is acceptable to governments because of the influence and expertise of the accountancy profession, which is usually running ahead of the interest of the government (in its capacity as shareholder, protector of public interest or collector of taxation). Thus, 'generally accepted accounting principles' control accounting. To the extent that governments intervene, they impose disclosure, filing or measurement requirements which tend to follow best practice rather than to create it.

In other European countries, banks, governments or families will nominate directors. Thus the major providers of finance have rapid access to detailed financial information. The traditional paucity of 'outsider' shareholders has meant that external financial reporting has been largely invented for the purposes of governments, as tax collectors or controllers of the economy. This has not encouraged the development of flexibility, judgment, fairness or experimentation.

As a counterpart to the above hypothesis, the following extreme idea may be formulated:

> In countries of continental Europe where most companies are heavily influenced by 'insiders', there will be little pressure for published accounts or for external audit.

This was approximately true until the late 1980s in Europe. For example, about a million UK companies had to publish audited accounts, whereas only public companies (ie about 2,200 AGs) and a few other very large companies had to do so in West Germany. Audit and publication were extended in Germany for 1987 year-ends as a result of the EC's Fourth Directive. However, newspaper reports suggest that most German GmbHs that have been supposed to file audited annual reports since 1987 have not done so. The penalties in German law are small and there is no commercial pressure for production and publication of audited reports.

Despite this great distinction, governments in most continental countries have recognised their responsibility to require public or listed companies to publish audited financial statements. This happened in a 1965 Act in West Germany; and in France and Italy the government has set up bodies specifically to control the securities markets: in France the *Commission des Opèrations de Bourse* (COB), and in Italy the *Commissione Nazionale per le Società e la Borsa* (CONSOB). These bodies are to some extent modelled on the Securities and Exchange Commission (SEC) of the USA. They have been associated with important developments in financial reporting, generally in the direction of Anglo-American practice. This is not surprising as these stock exchange bodies are taking the part of private and institutional shareholders who have, over a much longer period, helped to shape Anglo-American accounting systems.

In France the COB was formed in 1968. Its officers are appointed by the government. It is charged with encouraging the growth of the Bourse by improving the quality of published information and the operations of the market. It has established listing requirements and has investigated cases of non-compliance with publication and disclosure requirements. Perhaps its most obvious campaign was that to introduce consolidation. In 1968, consolidation was extremely rare, even for listed companies. Matters improved substantially under pressure from COB, including a requirement to consolidate for all companies wishing to obtain a new listing. This is discussed further in Chapter 2.

Although there are far fewer listed companies in Italy than there are in France (Italy does not even figure in Table 1.3), the effect of the CONSOB may be even greater than that of COB, partly because of the much less satisfactory state of affairs in Italy before CONSOB's formation in June 1974. CONSOB has powers to call for consolidation or extra disclosures which it has not used extensively yet. However, its real influence is linked to the Presidential Decree No 126 of March 1975 which, after much delay, was introduced by statutory instrument. This requires listed companies to have a more extensive audit, undertaken by an auditing company approved by

CONSOB. This requirement is in addition to the statutory audit by *sindaci* or state registered auditors.

1.4 Taxation

Although it is possible to make groupings of tax systems in a number of ways, only some of them are of relevance to financial reporting. For example, it is easy to divide EC countries into those using 'classical' and those using 'imputation' systems of corporation tax (Nobes and Parker, 1991, ch 20). However, this distinction does not affect financial reporting. What is much more relevant is the degree to which taxation regulations determine accounting measurements. To some extent this can be revealed in a negative way by studying the problem of deferred taxation, which is caused by timing differences between tax and accounting treatments. In the UK and the Netherlands (and the USA), for example, the problem of deferred tax has caused much controversy and a considerable amount of accounting standard documentation.

Turning to France or Germany, it is found that the problem does not really exist to be solved; for in these latter countries it is to a large extent the case that the tax rules *are* the accounting rules. In Germany, the commercial accounts (*Handelsbilanz*) should be the same as the tax accounts (*Steuerbilanz*). There is even a word for this idea: the *Massgeblichkeitsprinzip* (the principle of bindingness).

One obvious example of the effects of this concerns depreciation. In the UK, the amount of depreciation charged in the published financial statements is determined according to custom established over the last century and influenced by the accounting standard SSAP 12. The standard points out that:

> 'Depreciation should be allocated to accounting periods so as to charge a fair proportion of cost or valuation of the asset, to each accounting period expected to benefit from its use ... (para 3) ... Management should select the method regarded as most appropriate to the type of asset and its use in the business so as to allocate depreciation as fairly as possible....' (para 8).

These injunctions are of a fairly general nature, and their spirit is quite frequently ignored. Convention and pragmatism, rather than exact rules or even the spirit of the standard, also determine the method of judging the scrap value and the expected length of life.

The amount of depreciation *for tax purposes* in the UK is quite independent of these figures. It is determined by capital allowances, which are a formalised scheme of tax depreciation allowances designed to standardise the amounts allowed and to act as investment incentives. Because of the separation of the two schemes there can be a complete lack of subjectivity in tax allowances but full room for judgment in financial depreciation charges.

At the opposite extreme, in countries like Germany, the tax regulations lay down depreciation rates to be used for particular assets. These are generally based on the expected useful lives of assets. However, in some cases, accelerated depreciation allowances are available: for example, for industries producing energy-saving or anti-pollution products. Until the late 1980s, industries operating in West Berlin or other areas bordering East Germany received such allowances, which are now available in parts of Eastern Germany. If these allowances are to be claimed for tax purposes (which would normally be sensible), they must be charged in the financial accounts. Thus, the charge against profit would be said by a UK accountant not to be 'fair', even though it could certainly be 'correct' or 'legal'. This influence is felt even in the details of the choice of method of depreciation, as shown by an extract from the Annual Report of Daimler-Benz:

> 'For moveable property, we change from the declining-balance method to the straight-line method of calculating depreciation allowances when the equal distribution of the remaining net book value over the remaining useful life leads to higher depreciation amounts.' (1992, p 74).

A second example of the overriding effect of taxation on accounting measurement is the valuation of fixed assets in France. During the inflationary 1970s and before, French companies were allowed to revalue assets. However, this would have entailed extra taxation due to the increase in the post-revaluation balance sheet total compared to the previous year's. Consequently, except in the special case of merger by *fusion* when tax-exempt revaluation is allowed, revaluation was not practised. However, the Finance Acts of 1978 and 1979 made revaluation obligatory for listed companies and for those which solicit funds from the public; it was optional for others. The purpose was to show balance sheets more realistically. The revaluation was performed by the use of government indices relating to 31 December 1976. The credit went to an undistributable revaluation reserve. As a result of this, for depreciable assets, an amount equal to the extra depreciation due to revaluation is credited each year to profit and loss and *debited* to the revaluation account. Thus the effect of revaluation on profit (*and tax*) is neutralised. This move from no revaluations to compulsory revaluations was due to the change in tax rules. The effects spill over into the 1990s.

Somewhat similar tax-based revaluations have occurred in Italy, Greece and Spain. Further examples of the influence of tax are easy to find: bad debt provisions (determined by tax laws in many continental countries) or various provisions related to specific industries (see *Provisions and Reserves* in Chapter 2).

The effects of all this are to reduce the room for operation of the accruals convention (which is the driving force behind such practices as depreciation) and to reduce 'fairness'. Until the legislation following the EC's Fourth Directive, the importance of these tax effects was not disclosed in published accounts. With some variations, this *Massgeblichkeitsprinzip* operates in most continental countries except for the Netherlands. It is perhaps due partly to the persuasive influence of codification in law, and partly to the predominance of taxation as a cause of accounting.

The alternative approach is found in countries such as the UK, Ireland and the Netherlands, which have an older tradition of published accounting, where commercial rules have come first. Most of the countries on the left in Table 1.1 above, are, in varying degrees, like this. In most cases, there is not the degree of separation between tax and financial reporting that is found in the UK in the shape of capital allowances. However, in all such countries the taxation authorities have to adjust the commercial accounts for their own purposes, after exerting only minor influences directly on them. (For details on a major US exception to this rule, see Nobes, 1988.)

1.5 The Profession

The strength, size and competence of the accountancy profession in a country may follow to a large extent from the various factors outlined above and from the type of financial reporting they have helped to produce. For example, the lack of a substantial body of private shareholders and public companies in some countries means that the need for auditors is much smaller than it is in the UK (or the USA). However, the nature of the profession also feeds back into the type of accounting that is practised and *could* be practised. For example, as has been mentioned, the 1975 Decree in Italy (not brought into effect until the 1980s) requiring listed companies to have extended audits similar to those operated in the UK could only be brought into effect initially because of the substantial presence of international accounting firms. This constitutes a considerable obstacle to any attempts at significant and deep harmonisation of accounting between some countries. The need for extra auditors was a controversial issue in Germany's implementation of the EC's Fourth Directive.

The scale of the difference is illustrated in Table 1.4 opposite, which lists the bodies whose members may audit the accounts of companies (but see below for explanation of the French and German situation). These remarkable figures need some interpretation. For example, let us more carefully compare the German to the British figures. In Germany, there is a separate, though overlapping profession of tax experts (*Steuerberater*), which is larger than the accountancy body. However, in the UK the 'accountants' figure is especially inflated by the inclusion of many who specialise in or occasionally practise in tax. Secondly, a German accountant may only be a member of the *Institut* if he is in practice, whereas at least half of the British figure represents members in commerce, industry, government, education, and so on. Thirdly, the training period is much longer in Germany than it is in the UK. It normally involves a four-year relevant degree course, six years' practical experience (four in the profession), and a professional examination consisting of oral and written tests plus a thesis. This tends to last until the aspiring accountant is 30 to 35 years old. Thus, many of the German 'students' would be counted as part of the qualified figure if they were in the British system. In addition, in the late 1980s, Germany resuscitated a second-tier auditing body for the audit of private companies, the *Vereidigte Buchprüfer*.

These factors help to explain the differences. However, there is still a very substantial residual difference which results from the much larger number of companies to be audited.

It is interesting to note a further division along Anglo-American v Franco-German lines. In the former countries, governments or government agencies do require certain types of companies to be audited, and put certain limits on who shall be auditors, with government departments having the final say. However, in general, membership of the private professional accountancy bodies is the method of qualifying as an auditor. On the other hand, in France and Germany, there is a dual set of accountancy bodies. Those in Table 1.4 opposite are not the bodies to which one must belong to qualify as an auditor of companies, though to a large extent the membership of these professional bodies overlaps with the auditing bodies and membership of the former enables membership of the latter. The auditing bodies are shown in Table 1.5. The professional bodies set exams, consider ethical matters, belong to the international accounting bodies, and so on. The auditing

Table 1.4 Public Accountancy Bodies, Age and Size

Country	Body	Founding Date*	Approx. Nos in Thousands 1991/2
United States	American Institute of Certified Public Accountants	1887	301
Canada	Canadian Institute of Chartered Accountants	1902 (1880)	53
United Kingdom	Institute of Chartered Accountants in England and Wales	1880 (1870)	97
	Institute of Chartered Accountants of Scotland	1951 (1854)	13
	Chartered Association of Certified Accountants	1939 (1891)	38
	Institute of Chartered Accountants in Ireland	1888	8
Australia	Australian Society of Accountants	1952 (1887)	62
	Institute of Chartered Accountants in Australia	1928 (1886)	23
Netherlands	Nederlands Instituut van Registeraccountants	1895	8
France	Ordre des Experts Comptables et des Comptables Agréés	1942(1881)	12
Germany	Institut der Wirtschaftsprüfer	1932	6
Spain	Instituto de Censures Jurados de Cuentas	1945	6
	Registro de Economistas Auditores	1982	4
Japan	Japanese Institute of Certified Public Accountants	1948	10

*Dates of earliest predecessor bodies in brackets.

Table 1.5 Accountancy Bodies in France and Germany

	Private Professional Body	State Auditing Body
France	Ordre des Experts Comptables et des Comptables Agréés	Compagnie Nationale des Commissaires aux Comptes
Germany	Institut der Wirtschaftsprüfer	Wirtschaftsprüferkammer

bodies are run by the state. The *Compagnie Nationale* is responsible to the Ministry of Justice; the *Wirtschaftsprüferkammer* to the Federal Minister of Economics.

This split between professional, qualifying bodies and governmental, regulatory bodies was made an EC requirement by the Eighth Directive (adopted in 1984). The UK response to this (Companies Act 1989) was to allow certain self-regulatory bodies to control audit under the delegation of the Department of Trade and Industry. The self-regulatory bodies are none other than those qualifying bodies in Table 1.4!

1.6 Inflation

Accountants in the English-speaking world and governments in continental Europe have proved remarkably immune to inflation when it comes to decisive action. However, there are other countries where inflation has been overwhelming: in several South American countries, the most obvious feature of accounting practices is the use of methods of general price level adjustment (Tweedie and Whittington, 1984; Nobes and Parker, 1991, ch 16). The use of this comparatively simple method is probably due to the reasonable correlation of inflation with any particular specific price changes when the former is in hundreds of per cent per year; to the objective nature of government published indices; and to the paucity of well-trained accountants.

Without reference to this factor, it would not be possible to explain accounting differences in several countries severely affected by it. However, this factor is of only little assistance in explaining accounting differences in Europe. Nevertheless, the valuation of fixed assets particularly has been affected in some European countries, as discussed in section 2.5.

1.7 Theory

There has also been a strong influence in a few cases from theory, perhaps most obviously in the case of micro-economics in the Netherlands. Accounting theorists there (notably Theodore Limperg, Jr) had advanced the case that the users of financial statements would be given the fairest view of the performance and state of affairs of an individual company by allowing accountants to use judgment, in the context of that particular company, to select and present accounting figures. In particular, it was suggested that replacement cost information might give the best picture. The looseness of law and tax requirements, and the receptiveness of the profession to micro-economic ideas (no doubt partly because of their training by the academic theorists) has led to the present diversity of practice, the emphasis on 'fairness' through judgment, and the experimentation with and practice of replacement cost accounting.

In other countries, particularly in the English-speaking world, accounting practices seem to operate and develop without a clear theoretical framework. The standard-setters in the USA (the FASB) have been developing a conceptual framework since the middle 1970s, and there are more recent equivalents in the UK and Australia. However, standards are not yet consistent with these frameworks, and many practical choices still seem to be politically driven.

1.8 Accidents

Many other influences have been at work in shaping accounting practices. Some are not indirect and subtle like the type of ownership of companies, but direct and external to accounting like the framing of a law in response to economic or political events. As an example outside Europe, the economic crisis in the USA in the late 1920s and early 1930s produced the Securities and Exchange Acts which have diverted US accounting from its previous course by introducing extensive disclosure requirements and control (usually by threat only) of accounting standards. As other examples, the introductions into Italy of Anglo-American accounting principles by choice of the government, and into Luxembourg of consolidation and detailed disclosure as a result of EC Directives are against all previous trends there. In Spain, the 'artificial' adoption of the accounting plan from France follows that latter country's adoption of it after influence by the occupying Germans in the early 1940s. Perhaps most obvious and least natural is the adoption of various British Companies Acts or of International Accounting Standards by developing countries with a negligible number of the sort of public companies or private shareholders which have given rise to the financial reporting practices contained in these laws or standards. In its turn, the UK in 1981 enacted uniform formats derived from the 1965 *Aktiengesetz* of Germany because of EC requirements. For their part, Roman law countries are now having to grapple with the 'true and fair view' (see section 2.1).

1.9 A Note on Eastern Europe

It is now possible to say something concerning the former communist countries of Eastern Europe. Great progress has been made in many of these countries in the first half of the 1990s towards western-style capital markets. Many of them have passed laws modelled on the Fourth and Seventh Directives (see Chapter 4). To some extent western countries have been in competition to influence the development of accounting in Eastern Europe. Accountancy bodies and accountancy firms from the US and the UK have been vying with the French government and the traditional influence of German law and economic thinking.

Since there are few qualified accountants or listed companies, it is perhaps not surprising that a law-and-taxed-based system of a continental European style seems to be emerging in most Eastern European countries. However, the speed of change of the rules and the paucity of published annual reports of private sector companies makes any detailed description premature for the purposes of this book.

1.10 Summary and Conclusion

This chapter has discussed some of the influences on the development of European financial reporting practices. The importance of the mix of users of accounting information seems clear; it has a large part to play in the emergence of the dominant source of rules for accounting practice. In many continental European countries, the importance of governments as collectors of taxation or controllers of the economy, has led to the dominance of company laws, commercial codes and tax regulations. In other countries, the effective control of financial reporting practice has been exercised by the accounting profession. This was first seen as a vague corpus of 'best' or 'accepted' practices, and later has been refined with the issue of detailed accounting standards. However, these standards are still loosely-drawn documents which permit considerable flexibility and the use of judgment. The interests of private shareholders as users of financial statements has been a continuing background pressure on the profession as it develops standard practice.

As a result of international harmonisation, much of it directly caused by the EC, many European countries are finding 'fairness' and audit thrust upon them; and the UK, Ireland and the Netherlands are receiving many detailed financial reporting rules into law. This development cuts across the fundamental causes of differences that we have been looking at. However, at least before this influence was widely felt, it is clear that the same countries are generally found together for most of the factors discussed above. This observation leads on to the thought of classification of countries (see Chapter 3). At this point we might note that an interesting exception to the otherwise clear pattern of countries is the Netherlands. Although the Netherlands has a Roman legal system and few listed companies, if one studies its commercial, maritime history it bears considerable similarities to England's. Also, although the number of listed companies is small, some of those companies are very large and are the basis of an active stock exchange. At any rate, when it comes to taxation and the profession, the Netherlands appears to fit fairly well with the UK and Ireland (or the USA) as opposed to the continental European group.

References

Flint, D (1982) *A True and Fair View*, Gee, London.

Frank, W G (1979) 'An empirical analysis of international accounting principles', *Journal of Accounting Research*, Autumn.

Mueller, G G (1967) *International Accounting*, Macmillan, New York, part 1.

Nobes, C W (1986) 'New Laws for Old', *Accountancy*, December.

Nobes, C W and R H Parker (1991) *Comparative International Accounting*, Prentice Hall.

Nobes, C W (1988) Interpreting US Financial Statements, Butterworths.

Stamp, E (1980) *Corporate Reporting: Its Future Evolution*, Canadian Institute of Chartered Accountants, Toronto.

Tweedie, D P and G Whittington (1984) *The Debate on Inflation Accounting*, Cambridge University Press.

CHAPTER 2

European Differences in Financial Reporting

To some extent, differences in financial reporting have already been discussed in Chapter 1 while examining the causes of the differences. This applies particularly to the first two headings below, which are therefore dealt with briefly here. Also, it should be noted that many factors overlap with others. For example, a discussion of conservatism tends to overlap with discussions of the accruals convention or of fairness, because the former tends to drive out the others.

This chapter discusses the broad headings under which European differences in financial reporting may be found. More detail of specific practices is given in Chapters 5 to 8. The intention here is not primarily to examine accounting practices country by country; that is done elsewhere (eg Nobes and Parker, 1991).

2.1 Fairness

The degree to which accountants and auditors search for 'fairness' as opposed to correctness or legality has differed substantially internationally. This was discussed in Chapter 1 and was linked to (i) a predominance of outside shareholders as providers of finance, and (ii) the lack of interference of law or taxation in financial reporting.

Until the 1980s, the laws of the UK, Ireland and the Netherlands were alone in the EC in requiring fairness or faithfulness from audited financial statements. On the one hand this elevates judgment of particular circumstances above uniform rules, but on the other it can be a far more onerous requirement for directors and auditors. It can, of course, also lead to the abuse of flexibility by directors because of the vagueness of 'fair'.

A related concept is 'substance over form', an expression usually associated with the USA. In an attempt to 'present fairly', accountants have come to the view that it is necessary to try to account for the economic substance of events rather than for the legal form. For example, it is deemed necessary to capitalise assets obtained on finance leases as though they had been bought.

A concern with fairness also lies behind the Dutch experimentation and use of replacement cost valuation, and the agonised attempts in the English-speaking world since the late 1960s to replace or supplement historical cost accounting.

The requirement of the EC's Fourth Directive (see Chapter 4) that 'true and fair' should override detailed rules in all member states may lead to a mask of uniformity that conceals the unchanged old differences. For example, the requirement that French financial statements should give an *image fidèle* from 1984 involved changes in the law and in audit reports, but French accounting for individual companies seemed little altered.

Similarly, in West Germany, until 1987 financial statements there was still a requirement for fairness or for substance over form. Financial reporting was still an exercise in accurate bookkeeping which had to satisfy detailed rules and the scrutiny of the tax inspector. The recent requirement for French and German accounts to be 'fair' has largely been met by extra disclosures rather than a change in the presentation of numbers in the financial statements. This may make matters *worse* for Anglo-Saxon readers of financial statements, who may be misled by the increased superficial similarities.

2.2 Taxation

The influence of taxation has been discussed in Chapter 1 as a cause of differences in financial reporting. In most continental European countries, it is one of the enemies of fairness. In its effects on depreciation, bad debt provisions and some asset valuations it is a major example of differences in financial reporting.

2.3 Conservatism and Accruals

Another traditional adversary of fairness is conservatism. Perhaps because of the different mix of users in different countries, conservatism is of differing strengths. For example, the importance of banks in Germany may be a reason for greater conservatism in reporting. It is widely held that bankers are more interested in 'rock-bottom' figures in order to satisfy themselves that long-term loans are safe. At the same time, the consequent lack of those interested in a 'fair' view reduces the importance of the accruals convention which would normally modify conservatism.

In the UK it is now more usual to refer to the concept of 'prudence' (as in SSAP 2 and, now, company law). In many cases, accounting standards are the compromise treaties which settle a battle between conservatism and the accruals concept. For example, it is not fully conservative to allow the capitalisation of any development expenditure as in SSAP 13, but it may be reasonably prudent under certain conditions. A similar argument applies to the taking of profit on long-term contracts as in SSAP 9.

Continental European conservatism is of a more stringent variety, as may be illustrated by a study of published accounts. The evidence of conservatism in the following extracts depends upon the events of the year and the style of the companies' reports, thus it is not possible to organise a consistent survey. However, this report seems to be broadly representative of practice of large companies in Germany and is only presented as an example of the type of evidence available.

Daimler-Benz (1992)	Investments in related companies and in other long-term financial assets are valued at the lower of cost or market; non-interest bearing or low-interest bearing receivables are shown at their present value.

AEG (1988)	Raw materials are valued at cost of acquisition or at a lower value, to the extent that it is economically required or permissible.
Daimler-Benz (1992)	Foreign currency receivables are translated in the individual financial statements at the bid price on the day they are recorded or at the spot rate on the balance sheet date if lower. Foreign currency payables are translated at the asked price on the day they are recorded or the spot rate on the balance sheet date if higher.

By contrast, in the UK, long term investments are generally shown at cost unless there has been a permanent diminution in value. Receivables are not discounted to present value. Raw materials are not valued below cost or market. Foreign currency amounts are valued at the closing rate rather than some worse rate.

As a postscript, it may be noted that many investment analysts greatly increase a German company's profit figures by a series of adjustments before comparing it nationally or internationally (see occasional papers on Earnings per Share by *Deutsche Vereinigung für Finanzanalyse und Anlageberatung*). However, matters have 'improved' somewhat since the Aktiengesetz. Before that, it was suggested (Semler, 1962) that:

> 'If the non-existence of a contingency cannot be absolutely determined, then in the interest of protecting the creditor, it must be assumed that such a contingency exists.'

This greater conservatism in continental Europe seems to be a long-run phenomenon. Davidson and Kohlmeier (1966) and Abel (1969) noted that profit figures would be consistently lower in France, Sweden, Germany and the Netherlands (when use of replacement cost was assumed) if similar companies' accounts were merely adjusted for differences in inventory and depreciation practices from those used in the USA or the UK. Gray (1980) examined France, West Germany and the UK in order to produce an index of conservatism. He concluded that French and German companies are significantly more conservative or pessimistic than UK companies (p 69).

A further example of the protection of creditors is the use of statutory or legal reserves in most continental countries. These are undistributable reserves that are set up out of declared profits. They are an extra protection for creditors above the normal Anglo-American maintenance of capital rules. In France, Germany, Spain and Italy a company is required to appropriate 5% tranches (10% in Spain) of its annual profit until the statutory reserve reaches 10% of issued share capital (20% in Spain and Italy).

A particular piece of evidence of the lack of importance of the accruals concept (though not of conservatism) in many continental countries is the absence of a 'provision for proposed dividends' in annual balance sheets. Since there needs to be an AGM to bring the dividends into legal existence, they cannot exist at the balance sheet date! Some French balance sheets compromise between this and British views by presenting the liabilities-and-capital side of a balance sheet in two columns: before and after allocation of net profits.

There are some more remarks concerning conservatism and accruals in section 2.4 below.

2.4 Provisions and Reserves

The distinction between provisions and reserves is important for financial reporting because the former are charges against profit, whereas the latter are appropriations of profit. The influences which lead to a proliferation of significant provisions appear to be conservatism and rigid but generous tax regulations. Both these factors have been discussed, and their effects on provisions mentioned. The result of such provision-accounting may be that the accruals convention and 'fairness' are partially overridden; this in turn may result in income smoothing.

The use of accelerated depreciation in the financial accounts is an example of over-provision. The lack of provision for bad debts merely because it is not allowed for tax purposes is an example of under-provision. Provisions for risks and contingencies which fluctuate in reverse relationship with profits are examples of income smoothing. This will be illustrated using several different years of the annual reports of French and German companies.

In the 1983 Annual Report of CFP, there is a Chartered Accountants' Report (p A5) which notes that in the UK 'the provision for contingencies would be classified as a reserve'. In earlier years, there were even more revealing remarks in the versions of the annual reports of CFP that were specially prepared for UK readers:

> 'Depreciation of property, plant and equipment was F 2274 million vs F 2283 million in 1976. Provision amounts were lower in 1977 than in 1976, especially because cash flow reflected on the French market did not allow constitution of a provision for foreign exchange fluctuations at the same level as in 1976.' (1977, p 22)

> 'Taking into account these items, income for the year was F 111 million, to which must be added a deduction of F 90 million from the provision for contingencies. Income finally amounts to F 201 million ... but includes lower exceptional income.' (1977, p 23)

> 'Following the usual effect of amounts set aside to or written back from depreciation and provisions and an allocation of F 800 million to reconstitute the provision for contingencies, net income for the year totalled F 971 million.' (1979, p 23)

As a result of the 1983 Law requiring fairness, CFP transferred its contingency 'provision' to 'reserves' in 1984. However, not all large French companies have followed this practice.

Turning to Germany, remarks concerning provisions have already been made in the section on conservatism. Using AEG again as an example, the 1987 profit and loss account (see Table 2.1 opposite) shows a 'net income' of exactly zero for 1986 and 1987. The inevitable conclusion must be that the income statement is calculated by working backwards from the 'net income' of zero. This is income smoothing on an heroic scale. More recently, Daimler-Benz (1991) Annual Report notes that: 'The income amount

Table 2.1 Consolidated Statement of Income of AEG Group for 1987

	1987		1986	
	Million DM	**Million DM**	**Million DM**	**Million DM**
Sales	**11,660**		**11,220**	
Change in inventories and work capitalised	+ 276		+ 137	
Total Operating Performance		**11,936**		**11,357**
Other operating income	+ 533		+ 464	
Cost of materials	− 5,376		− 5,212	
Personnel expenses	− 4,642		− 4,489	
Depreciation of intangible and fixed assets	− 357		− 295	
Other operating expenses	− 2,050		− 1,760	
Investment results (net)	+ 16		+ 2	
Interest income (net)	+ 26		+ 1	
Result from other financial investments and current assets securities (net)	− 3			
		−11,853		**−11,289**
Results from Ordinary Business Activity		**+ 83**		**+ 68**
Extraordinary results	− 19		—	
Taxes on income	− 16		− 25	
Other taxes	− 48		− 43	
		− 83		**− 68**
Net Income		−		−
Withdrawals from transfers to revenue reserves	+ 5		− 12	
Minority interest in income and losses	− 5		+ 12	
Group Result		−		−

included in [Other Operating Income] for the reversal of provisions totals DM 893 million.' This is in the context of group income for the year of DM 1942 million. In 1993, Daimler-Benz announced that hidden reserves/provisions of DM 4 billion would be explained. This case is looked at further in Chapter 9.

It appears that, in Italy and Spain, the Commercial Codes (which would certainly allow greater use of the accruals convention) have been overridden to a large extent by the need to satisfy the requirements of tax inspectors. Only recently, have tax reforms and stronger accounting principles allowed the use of 'fairer' provisions of various types.

In the UK, provisions for depreciation and for non-specific bad debts are not affected by tax requirements. Provisions for risks and contingencies are rare and usually associated with cases where a liability is specifically identified and probable. Broadly speaking, these practices prevail in the rest of the English-speaking world and in the Netherlands and Denmark. However, there is an important exception in the treatment of deferred tax, which is fully provided for in the USA, Canada, Australia, and the Netherlands, but (since the late 1970s) not in the UK and Ireland (see Chapter 7).

2.5 Valuation Bases

There is great international variation in the predominant basis of valuation and the degree to which there is experimentation and supplementation with alternative measures. In a country with detailed legal rules and a coincidence of tax and commercial accounting it must be expected that the predominant valuation system will be one that involves as little judgment as possible. Flexibility and judgment would make it difficult for auditors to determine whether the law had been obeyed and they might lead to arbitrary taxation demands. Thus, in a country such as Germany, it seems unsurprising that the required method of valuation is a strict form of historical cost.

At the other extreme is the Netherlands. Some Dutch companies (eg Philips) have published replacement cost financial statements since the early 1950s. Although this remains minority practice, many Dutch companies partially or supplementarily use replacement costs or other current values. Dutch practice reflects the influence of microeconomic theory and a striving after fairness.

In between these two extremes, UK 'rules' allow a chaotic state of affairs where some companies revalue, some of the time, using a variety of methods. Also, there has been experimentation with current cost accounting, normally as supplementary statements. This is the story for most of the English-speaking world, except that the USA and Canada keep to historical cost in the main financial statements; this is because of the influence of the SEC.

In France, Spain, Greece and Italy, where there is much tax and other government influence, there has also been more inflation than in Germany and a greater drive towards the creation of large and efficient equity capital markets. Governments and stock exchange bodies in these countries have appreciated the effects of inflation on historical cost accounting and have required revaluations. However, this creates severe problems in such countries (see Chapter 6).

This fundamental difference in methods of asset valuation means that international comparisons become difficult for net assets, shareholders' funds and many ratios.

2.6 Consolidation

The prevalence of consolidation has varied dramatically among EC countries. Most practices seem to have first enjoyed widespread adoption in the USA: for example, the normal acquisition (purchase) method of accounting for a business combination. There are examples of consolidation at least as far back as the 1890s, and it was widespread practice by the early 1920s. The various factors that might have caused this early development in the USA may help to explain the diversity in the EC. The US factors may have been:

(*i*) a wave of mergers at the turn of the century, leading to the carrying on of business by groups of companies;
(*ii*) the prevalence of the holding company (which merely owns investments) as opposed to the parent company (which is one of the operating companies of the group);
(*iii*) the lack of a legal requirement for holding/parent company balance sheets, unlike the UK or German law for example;
(*iv*) the lack of legal or other barriers to the emergence of new techniques, and the existence of innovative professionals;
(*v*) use of consolidation for tax purposes (1917 to 1934);
(*vi*) acceptance of consolidation by the New York Stock Exchange (1919).

In the UK consolidation came later. Holding companies were perhaps less important until during the First World War, although there was a UK wave of mergers at the turn of the century. Nevertheless, UK mergers did not usually involve holding companies. Also, tax never moved to a consolidated basis in the UK. It used to be commonly held that Nobel Industries (ICI) pioneered consolidation in the early 1920s and Dunlop in the 1930s. However, Edwards and Webb (1984) have found much earlier evidence. The Stock Exchange required consolidation as a condition of new issues from 1939; and consolidation became almost universal after the Companies Act 1948.

In the Netherlands, consolidation was also practised by the 1930s. However, in most of continental Europe, consolidation is either a recent development or still very rare. In Germany, consolidation was made obligatory by the 1965 *Aktiengesetz* for public (AG) companies. However, foreign subsidiaries did not need to be (and generally were not) consolidated, and the use of the equity method for associated companies was not allowed. Further, there were important differences from Anglo-American practice in the use of an economic (rather than a legal) basis for 'the group', and a yearly calculation of 'differences arising on consolidation' based on book values rather than a once-for-all calculation of goodwill based on fair values. Germany implemented the Seventh Directive in 1985, thus removing most of these differences from 1990 (see Chapter 8).

In France, before 1985, there was no law on consolidation, and consolidation had been very rare. However, the formation of COB in the late 1960s and the influence of Anglo-American practices, due to the presence of international firms and the desire of some French companies for listings on

Table 2.2 Number of Listed French Companies Publishing Consolidated Financial Statements

	At least a consolidated balance sheet	**Consolidated balance sheet plus consolidated profit and loss account**
1967	22	15
1968	44	25
1969	64	39
1970	74	42
1971	104	76
1972	163	121
1973	216	161
1974	232	183
1975	267	213
1976	292	246
1977	319	267
1978	328	289
1979	351	305

Source: Commission des Opérations de Bourse, Annual Reports.

the Exchanges of London or New York, caused a gradual increase in consolidation by listed companies (see Table 2.2 above). Naturally, in a country where there is no tradition of professional accounting measurement standards, in cases where there were no law or tax requirements, practice has been very varied. The *Conseil National de la Comptabilité*, a government body with responsibility for the *Plan*, issued guidelines in 1968 and 1978. However, these guidelines were not followed exactly. In 1985 a law was passed to require listed companies to publish consolidated financial statements by 1987. Other companies had to follow by 1989.

In Belgium, Italy and Spain, until the 1980s, consolidation was very rare. In Portugal, it was unknown. The result of lack of consolidation in these many EC countries is that outside investors or lenders (particularly foreigners) have grossly inadequate information, even about large listed groups. The situation in Switzerland was broadly the same. Tables 2.3 and 2.4 opposite show the best available set of accounts for a large Swiss group in the late 1980s. It appears that there are no buildings or machines, no sales or wages. This is because the best available accounts are those of the holding company, whereas all the operations are performed in subsidiaries. Of course, it is even more confusing when *part* of the group's operations is performed by the parent. In Switzerland, consolidation became compulsory as a result of a law of 1991 for AGs whose groups exceed two of the following criteria:

Turnover:	SF 20 million
Balance sheet:	SF 10 million
Employees:	200

Why have most continental European countries been so far behind the UK and the USA in the development of consolidation? The reasons may include:

Table 2.3 Balance Sheet of Holzstoff Holding Inc at 31.12.1986

		SFr
Assets	Investments	73 523 170.—
	Loans to group companies	33 068 800.—
	Accounts receivable	2 839 436.34
	Securities	3 328 330.—
	Cash and cash items	46 399 694.46
	Total	159 159 430.80
Liabilities and equity	Share capital	40 000 000.—
	Legal reserves	4 840 000.—
	Special reserves	22 200 000.—
	Debentures* 4 1/2, due 1992	15 000 000.—
	4 3/4, due 1993	20 000 000.—
	Accounts payable	138 476.80
	Provisions	48 209 590.—
	Retained earnings	282 860.36
	Earnings	8 488 503.64
	Total	159 159 430.80

Table 2.4 Income Statement of Holzstoff Holding Inc for 1986

		SFr
Revenues	Revenue from investments	12 437 023.13
	Interest income	2 967 437.96
	Other revenue	388 249.95
	Dissolution of the provision for cost of group reorganisation	—
	Total	15 792 711.04
Expenditures	Interest expense	1 625 000.—
	Taxes	1 646 207.40
	Depreciation and provisions	4 033 000.—
	Cost of group reorganisation	—
	Earnings	8 488 503.64
	Total	15 792 711.04

(*i*) the existence of many legal requirements that made the preparation of individual company balance sheets compulsory and militated against new ideas;
(*ii*) the lack of a large or strong profession to innovate;
(*iii*) the lesser importance of big business and holding companies;
(*iv*) the importance of bankers and creditors who might oppose consolidation on the grounds that it confuses legal liabilities;
(*v*) the importance (as users of accounts) of the revenue authorities, and in some cases governments, who prefer to do their own manipulations of the accounts of individual companies;
(*vi*) the relative lack of importance of shareholders who may want an overall 'economic' view.

One of the effects of this rarity of consolidation was that the EC's major draft law on financial reporting (the Fourth Directive) was adopted in 1978 without any recognition of group accounting. Presumably, when the first draft was published in 1971, a requirement to consolidate would have been hopelessly controversial.

However, as we have seen, the stock exchange bodies and governments of most EC countries have begun to take actions to require listed or public companies to consolidate. This is designed to make their domestic capital markets more efficient and to internationalise the flows of capital. It is of course logical to direct the consolidation rules at those companies where outside providers of finance are important. The Seventh Directive of the EC (adopted in 1983) required consolidation rules by 1990 (see Chapter 8).

2.7 Uniformity and Accounting Plans

The degree to which financial reporting is uniform among companies within a country varies. Before the early 1980s when the EC's harmonising measures began to take effect, the variations were greater. Uniformity can exist in three main areas: formats of financial statements, accounting principles and disclosure requirements. Clearly, where there are detailed legal rules in any or all of these areas, there will be a high degree of uniformity.

In order to examine the emergence of uniformity, one should probably start with Germany. It was for internal, cost accounting purposes that uniform formats were first developed. They could also be used for inter-firm comparisons within an industry. It appears that the first comprehensive chart of accounts was published in Germany in 1911 and that such charts were used by industry in the First World War. Under the National Socialists, the ascendant ideology of controlling the economy led naturally to the compulsory adoption of charts of accounts.

In France, the needs of the Economics Ministry in its role as controller of the French economy were seen to be well served by the use of uniform accounting encouraged by the occupying German forces in the early 1940s. Consequently, such a system has been in use in France throughout the post-war years. The first full version of the *plan comptable général* was produced in 1947, and revised versions were issued in 1957 and (as partial implementation of the Fourth Directive) in 1982. The *plan* exists in many versions for different industries. It comprises a chart of accounts, definitions of terms, model financial statements and rules for measurement and valuation. The chart of accounts controls a company's internal bookkeeping system. It is a decimalised system of nominal ledger codes. The first two digits of the current French chart are shown in Table 2.5 on p 26. However, the detail goes down to five digits. This system makes work easier for auditors, tax inspectors and accountants as they move from one company to another. It also speeds the training of bookkeepers; and it is an obvious micro-computer application.

The influence of the *plan comptable* is all-pervasive. The chart must be completed each year for national statistical purposes; the tax returns are based on the plan; published financial statements use the model formats (see Chapter 5); and all the former use the standard definitions and measurement rules. The *plan* even stretches to cost and management accounting.

Its use for central statistical purposes is very obvious. A government economist in Paris can collect charts for all companies and add together all amounts under a particular decimalised code in order to find the total investment in a particular type of fixed asset, defined in a standardised way. Naturally, as the government is historically the main user of accounting information in its capacities as economic controller, tax collector and provider of state capital, the *plan* is controlled by a government body: the *Conseil National de la Comptabilité*. It is enforced through a company law of 1983. The plan was revised in 1985 to take account of the group accounting rules of the EC Seventh Directive.

In Belgium, part of the process of preparing for the implementation of the Fourth Directive during the 1970s was the introduction of an accounting plan in 1976, not dissimilar to the French one. The Belgians had used a chart of accounts for some industries during the inter-war years, and had experienced full use of it during the early 1940s. The *plan comptable minimum normalisé* is now compulsory. However, unlike the French *plan*, the Belgian one mainly concerns charts of accounts, which are to be sent to the Banque Nationale.

In Spain, an accounting plan has been progressively introduced. The Ministry of Public Finance established the Institute of Accounting Planning in 1973 which has produced several versions of the plan for different sectors. As in France, the plan consists of a chart of accounts, a set of definitions, formats for annual accounts and valuation principles. The headings of the decimalised chart of accounts are in the same order as the French chart, though the subheadings vary to some extent. The plan began by being voluntary. Then, by an Act of December 1973, the plan had to be used for those companies who wished to revalue. This continued for the 1978 and 1979 fiscal revaluations (somewhat like the French revaluations of similar date). However, by an Order of 14 January 1980, companies covered by plans already in issue must now comply with the plans.

Greece has also adopted an accounting plan. In this case, and in France and Spain, the *plans* include uniform financial statements for publication. In Belgium and Germany, uniform financial statements are required instead by company law. An interesting irony is that Germany is now the only country of the five not to have a compulsory accounting plan.

In Anglo-Saxon countries, there has generally been much less uniformity. As far as formats for financial statements are concerned, there were no rules in law (before the 1981 UK Act and the 1983 Netherlands Act) and virtually none in accounting standards. The requirements of the Fourth Directive were based on German law and were revolutionary compared to previous

Table 2.5 Extract from French Chart of Accounts

Balance sheet accounts					Management accounts		Special Accounts	COST ACCOUNTING
Class 1	**Class 2**	**Class 3**	**Class 4**	**Class 5**	**Class 6**	**Class 7**	**Class 8**	**Class 9**
Capital accounts (capital, loans and similar creditors)	Fixed asset accounts	Stock and work-in progress accounts	Personal accounts	Financial accounts	Expense accounts	Income accounts	Special accounts	Cost accounts
10 Capital and reserves	20 Intangible assets	30	40 Suppliers and related accounts	50 Trade investments	60 Purchases and stock movements (supplies and goods for resale)	70 Sales of goods and	80 Contingent assets and liabilities	90 Reciprocal accounts
11 Profit or loss brought forward	21 Tangible assets	31 Raw materials	41 Trade debtors and related accounts	51 Banks financial and similar institutions	61 Purchases from sub-contractors and external charges (related to investment)	71 Movements in finished goods during the accounting period	81[(a)]	91 Cost reclassifications
12 Profit or loss for the financial year	22 Fixed assets under concession	32 Other consumables	42 Employees and related accounts	52	62 Other external charges (related to operations)	72 Work performed by the undertaking for its own purposes and capitalised	82[(a)]	92 Cost analysis centres
13 Investment grants	23 Fixed assets in course of construction	33 Work in progress (goods)	43 Social security and other public agencies	52 Cash in hand	63 Taxes, direct and indirect	73 Net income recognised on long-term contracts	83[(a)]	93 Manufacturing costs

14 Provisions created for tax purposes	24	34 Work-in progress (services)	44 The Government and other public bodies	54 Imprest accounts and credits	64 Staff costs	74 Operating subsidies	84[(a)]	94 Stocks
15 Provisions for liabilities and charges	25	35 Finished goods	45 Accounts current—group companies and proprietors	55	65 Other operating charges	75 Other operating income	85[(a)]	95 Costs of goods sold
16 Loans and similar creditors	26 Participating interests and debts relating thereto	36	46 Sundry debtors and creditors	56	66 Financial costs	76 Financial income	86 Intra-company exchanges of goods and services (charges)	96 Standard cost variances
17 Debts related to participa-interests	27 Other financial assets	37 Goods for resale	47 Suspense accounts	57 Internal transfers	67 Extra-ordinary	77 Extra-ordinary	87 Intra-company exchanges of goods and services (income)	97 Difference in accounting treatments
18 Branch and inter company accounts	38 Provisions for depreciation of fixed assets	38	48 Prepayments and accruals	58	68 Depreciation amortisation, transfers to provisions	78 Depreciation and provisions written back	88	98 Manufacturing profit and loss account
19	29 Provisions for loss in value of fixed assets	39 Provisions for loss in value of stocks and work-in progress	49 Provisions for loss in value on personal accounts	59 Provisions for loss in value on financial accounts	69 Profit sharing by employees, taxes on profits and similar items	79 Charges transferred	89	99 Internal transfers

Anglo-Dutch rules. But even now, there remains much more flexibility in the UK, Ireland and the Netherlands than in the rest of the EC.

Turning to accounting principles, the control by company law, tax law or accounting plan has been substantial in most EC countries. Though, again, in the UK, Ireland and the Netherlands, there have traditionally been no rules in company law apart from 'fairness'. Instead, the accountancy profession has been influential in inventing and policing the rules of valuation and measurement. In the UK and Ireland, the Accounting Standards Committee is controlled by the professional bodies. In the Netherlands, guidelines are published by the Council for Annual Reporting (*Raad voor de Jaarverslaggeving*) in which the Netherlands Institute of Registered Accountants plays the most influential role.

Standards and guidelines in these latter countries are not part of law. In the UK and Ireland, non-compliance should lead to an audit qualification; in the Netherlands not even that. However, the legal requirement for 'fairness' would be likely to be interpreted by a court with the aid of standards. In the UK, standards were mentioned in the Companies Act 1989 and have some legal status, particularly for listed companies and other large public companies whose directors are required to state whether the annual report complies with accounting standards. In the Netherlands there is a special Enterprise Chamber of the Court of Justice especially for accounting cases. Nevertheless, there has been plenty of room for variety in those Anglo-Saxon countries in the EC and elsewhere. However, the implementation of the Fourth Directive has introduced many detailed rules into law for the first time. This has somewhat increased uniformity, but mainly it has raised problems between law and standards.

The remaining potential area of uniformity is disclosure requirements. One difference between Franco-German and Anglo-Saxon practice is that companies in the former countries tend to restrict their disclosures to legal requirements, except when seeking to raise Anglo-American finance. In the UK and Ireland, the basic disclosures required by law are substantial and lead to considerable uniformity. However, other disclosures required by or recommended by the profession, or experimented with by individual companies, are common. This leads to a certain degree of variation.

2.8 Shareholder Orientation of Financial Statements

The first section of this chapter discussed the connection between 'fairness' and the predominance of outside shareholders. Shareholder orientation spreads further than accounting principles; it affects the formats of financial statements. At its most obvious, the general use of a vertical format of the balance sheet in the UK and Ireland rather than a horizontal format in Germany or France suggests a greater shareholder-orientation in the former countries. This is because the vertical format allows the presentation of working capital and net worth, and it contrasts net worth with shareholders' funds.

However, even in the horizontal version of the balance sheet (see Chapter 5), the UK version has greater shareholder-orientation than a traditional German, Spanish or Italian format: for example, it shows all the elements of shareholders' funds together, rather than showing the year's net profit as a separate item at the bottom of the balance sheet (or a loss at the bottom of the assets side!) as did the 1965 *Aktiengesetz*. The greater German interest in the double-entry aspects of the balance sheet was also demonstrated by the presentation of 'provisions for bad debts' as a liability (rather than being deducted from debtors), and 'called up share capital not paid' as the first asset (rather than as a debtor). The formats introduced in Germany by the 1985 legislation to implement the Fourth Directive removed many of these differences, but other continental countries still retained them (eg Spain until 1990 and Italy until 1993).

The usual German style profit and loss account (see Chapter 5) is also probably less useful for decision-making than the normal Anglo-Saxon concentration on gross profit, net profit and 'earnings'. This is in addition to the problem of income smoothing discussed earlier. Further, disclosed calculations of earnings per share are not normal in most of continental Europe.

2.9 Conclusion

The eight areas of difference discussed above are amongst the more important variations in financial reporting practice, though they do not amount to a complete list. What is clear is that a reader would be seriously misled if he or she compared financial statements from apparently similar companies from various countries. The first step is to be aware that the differences exist. Later chapters suggest adjustments that might be made.

References

Abel, R (1969) 'A comparative simulation of German and US accounting principles', *Journal of Accounting Research*, Spring.

Davidson, S and Kohlmeier, J (1966) 'A measure of the impact of some foreign accounting principles', *Journal of Accounting Research*, Autumn.

Edwards, J R and Webb, K M (1984) 'The development of group accounting in the UK to 1933', *Accounting Historians Journal*, Spring.

Gray, S J (1980) 'The impact of international accounting differences from a security-analysis perspective: some European evidence', *Journal of Accounting Research*, Spring.

Nobes, C W and Parker, R H (1991) *Comparative International Accounting*, Prentice Hall.

Semler, J (1962) 'The German accountant's approach to safeguarding investors' and creditors' interests', paper at the Eighth International Congress of Accountants, reprinted in *The Australian Accountant*, September.

CHAPTER 3

Classification of Financial Reporting in Europe

Chapters 1 and 2 have discussed the causes and main examples of differences in financial reporting practices in Europe. From this it is clear that, although no two countries have identical rules and practices, some countries seem to form pairs or larger groupings with reasonably similar financial reporting. If this is so, it may be possible to establish a classification. Such an activity is a basic step in many disciplines other than accounting. Before attempting a European accounting classification, it may be useful to make short surveys of classification in other disciplines, of the normal rules for classifications, of the purposes of classifications, and of previous attempts in accounting.

3.1 Purpose, Rules and Examples

Classification is one of the basic tools of a scientist. The Mendeleev table of elements and the Linnaean system of classification are fundamental to chemistry and biology. Classification should sharpen description and analysis. It should reveal underlying structures and enable prediction of the properties of an element based on its place in a classification.

Different types of classification are possible, from the simplest form of dichotomous grouping (eg things black versus things white) or rank ordering (eg by height of students in a class) to more complex dimensioning (such as the periodic table) or systematising (such as the Linnaean system).

It may now be useful to examine traditional methods of classification in areas close to accounting. There have been classifications of political, economic and legal systems. For example, political systems have been grouped into political democracies, tutelary democracies, modernising oligarchies, totalitarian oligarchies and traditional oligarchies. Economic systems have been divided into capitalism, socialism, communism and fascism. A more recent classification is: traditional economies, market economies and planned economies.

One set of authors, while classifying legal systems, has supplied practical criteria for determining whether two systems are in the same group. Systems are said to be in the same group if 'someone educated in . . . one law will then be capable, without much difficulty, of handling (the other)' (David and Brierley, 1978, p 20). Also, the two systems must not be 'founded on opposed philosophical, political or economic principles'. The second criterion ensures that systems in the same group not only have superficial characteristics, but also have similar fundamental structures and are likely to react to new circumstances in similar ways. Using these criteria a four-group legal classification was obtained: Romano-Germanic, Common Law, Socialist and Philosophical-Religious.

In all the above examples, the type of classification used was rudimentary, involving no more than splitting systems into a few groups. The groups within the classifications were sometimes not precisely defined nor exhaustive. Also, the method used to determine and fill the groups was little more than subjective classification based on personal knowledge or descriptive literature. These shortcomings are very difficult to avoid because of the complexity and 'greyness' in the social sciences.

3.2 Classification in Accounting

The reasons for wanting to classify financial reporting 'systems' into groups include the general reasons for classification in any science, as outlined above. In this case, classification should be an efficient way of describing and comparing different systems. It should help to chart the progress of one system as it moves from one group to another, and the progress of ideas of a dominant country's system, by noting the other national systems grouped around it. The activity involved in preparing a classification should encourage precision. Moreover, in the social sciences, classification may be used to help shape development rather than merely to describe how and why things are. For example, classification should facilitate a study of the logic of and the difficulties facing European harmonisation. Classification should also assist in the training of accountants and auditors who operate internationally. Further, a developing country might be better able to understand the available types of financial reporting, and which one would be most appropriate for it, by seeing which other countries use particular systems. Also, it should be possible for a country to predict the problems that it is about to face and the solutions that might work by looking at other countries in its group.

Early Classification and Recent Descriptions

Early attempts at classification and more recent descriptions of different national systems form the background to modern classifications. Of the former, there is evidence for a three-group classification (UK, US and continental) being used from the beginning of the twentieth century (Hatfield, reprinted 1966). More recent descriptions and analyses like those by Zeff (1972), Price Waterhouse (1973, 1975 and 1979) and the AICPA (1964 and 1975) provide the raw material for classification.

Mueller's Classification

Mueller (1967) broke new ground by preparing a suggested classification of accounting systems into four patterns of development. This was a simple grouping which is not accompanied by an explanation of the method used to obtain it. However, the 'range of four is considered sufficient to embrace accounting as it is presently known and practised in various parts of the globe' (Mueller 1967, p 2). Each group was illustrated by one or two examples. It may well be that it is not reasonable to expect a more sophisticated classification, particularly in a pioneering work, and that Mueller's informed judgment was one of the best methods of classification available.

Mueller stresses that the types of accounting rules which exist in a country are a product of economic, political and other environments, which have determined the nature of the system. This also suggests that other countries' rules would not be appropriate to that country and that rules must be chosen to fit a country's needs. Consequently, doubt is cast on the possibility and usefulness of harmonisation.

Mueller's four groups, which are usefully summarised in a later work (Choi and Mueller 1984) are:

1 **Accounting within a Macroeconomic Framework.** In this case, accounting has developed as an adjunct of national economic policies. We might expect such financial accounting to stress value-added statements, to encourage income smoothing, to be equivalent to tax accounting and to include social responsibility accounting. Sweden is said to be an example.

2 **The Microeconomic Approach.** This approach can prosper in a market-oriented economy which has individual private businesses at the core of its economic affairs. The influence of microeconomics has led accounting to try to reflect economic reality in its measurement and valuations. This means that accounting rules must be sophisticated but flexible. Developments like replacement cost accounting will be accepted most readily in such systems. The Netherlands is suggested as an example.

3 **Accounting as an Independent Discipline.** Systems of this sort have developed independently of governments or economic theories. Accounting has developed in business, has faced problems when they arrived, and has adopted solutions which worked. Theory is held in little regard and turned to only in emergencies or used *ex post* in an attempt to justify practical conclusions. Expressions such as 'generally accepted accounting principles' are typical. Mueller recognised the accounting systems of the UK and the USA as examples.

4 **Uniform Accounting.** Such systems have developed where government have used accounting as a part of the administrative control of business. Accounting can be used to measure performance, allocate funds, assess the size of industries and resources, control prices, collect taxation, manipulate sectors of business, and so on. It involves standardisation of definitions, measurements and presentation. France is cited as an example.

Mueller was not classifying financial reporting systems directly, on the basis of differences in *practices*, but indirectly, on the basis of differences in the importance of economic, governmental and business factors in the development of particular systems. However, one might expect that systems which have developed in a similar way would have similar accounting practices.

Nevertheless, there are a few problems with Mueller's classification. The fact that there are only four exclusive groups and no hierarchy reduces the usefulness of the classification. In effect, the Netherlands is the only country in one of the groups and the classification does not show whether Dutch accounting is closer to UK accounting than it is to Swedish accounting. Similarly, the classification cannot include such facts as that German accounting exhibits features which remind one of macroeconomic accounting as well as of uniform accounting.

Spheres of Influence

There have been some 'subjective' classifications based on 'spheres of influence'. Seidler (1967) suggested three groups: British, American and continental European. Also, the AAA's committee produced a subjective classification of 'zones of influence' on accounting systems (AAA 1977, pp 105 and 129–130). These are:

1 British
2 Franco-Spanish-Portuguese
3 German-Dutch
4 US
5 Communist

This classification is perhaps most useful in a discussion of developing countries. It seems less appropriate as a general method of classifying financial reporting. This is because it has no hierarchy and thus does not take account, for example, of the links between British and US accounting. Further, to call a group 'German–Dutch' seems very inappropriate as a way of classifying developed financial reporting systems, when examined in the light of the material in Chapters 1 and 2.

Classifications using Clustering

Other researchers have used the 1973 and the 1975 Price Waterhouse Surveys. For example, Nair and Frank (1980) divide the 1973 Survey's financial reporting characteristics into those relating to measurement and those relating to disclosure. This is a very useful differentiation, particularly because of the effect it has on the classification of countries like Germany which have advanced disclosure requirements. Using disclosure and measurement characteristics, Germany is classified in a 'US group'. However, by using 'measurement' characteristics only, Nair and Frank (1980) classify Germany in the continental European group. Table 3.1 below

Table 3.1 Classification Based on Measurement Practices

British Commonwealth Model	**Latin American Model**	**Continental European Model**	**United States Model**
Australia	Argentina	Belgium	Canada
Bahamas	Bolivia	France	Japan
Eire	Brazil	Germany	Mexico
Fiji	Chile	Italy	Panama
Jamaica	Columbia	Spain	Philippines
Kenya	Ethiopia	Sweden	United States
Netherlands	India	Switzerland	
New Zealand	Paraguay	Venezuela	
Pakistan	Peru		
Rhodesia	South Africa		
Singapore	Uruguay		
Trinidad & Tobago			
United Kingdom			

Source: Nair and Frank (1980).

represents the classification using measurement characteristics. As yet there is no hierarchy, but the overall results do seem very plausible and fit well with the analysis in previous chapters of this book.

The suggestion is that, in a world-wide context, much of continental Europe can be seen as using the same system. However, the UK, Ireland and the Netherlands are noticeably different.

3.3 A New Approach

It would be possible to criticise the classifications discussed above for: (i) lack of precision in the definition of what is to be classified; (ii) lack of a model with which to compare the statistical results; (iii) lack of hierarchy which would add more subtlety to the portrayal of the size of differences between countries; and (iv) lack of judgment in the choice of 'important' discriminating features. Can these problems be remedied? The author attempted to solve them in his own researches relating to 14 developed countries (see Table 3.2 opposite and Nobes, 1983). This approach is adapted here for the 12 countries of the EC. (As may be seen from Table 3.2, the original study included the following EC countries: UK, Ireland, Netherlands, Belgium, France, Germany, Italy and Spain.)

Definition

The scope of the work is defined as the classification of some European countries by the financial reporting practices of their *public companies*. The reporting practices are those concerned with *measurement and valuation*. It is public companies whose financial statements are generally available and whose practices can be most easily discovered. It is the international differences in reporting between such companies which are of main interest to shareholders, creditors, auditing firms, taxation authorities, managements and harmonising agencies. Measurement and valuation practices were chosen because these determine the size of the figures for profit, capital, total assets, liquidity and so on.

A Model with a Hierarchy

The hypothetical classification shown as Table 3.3 on p 36 is adapted from that proposed for a somewhat different group of countries in the previous study. The classification is based on the major background factors of law, tax and predominant users.

Classifications by others (eg Table 3.1) have contained separate groups but no hierarchy which would indicate the comparative distances between the groups. It may well be reasonable to classify the UK and the Netherlands in different groups, but it might be useful to demonstrate that these two groups are closely linked, compared to, say, continental European countries. The classification in Table 3.3 contains a hierarchy which borrows its labels from biology.

Table 3.3 suggests that there are two main types of financial reporting 'system' in Europe: the micro/professional and the macro/uniform. The

Table 3.2 A Hypothetical Classification of Financial Reporting Measurement Practices in Developed Western Countries

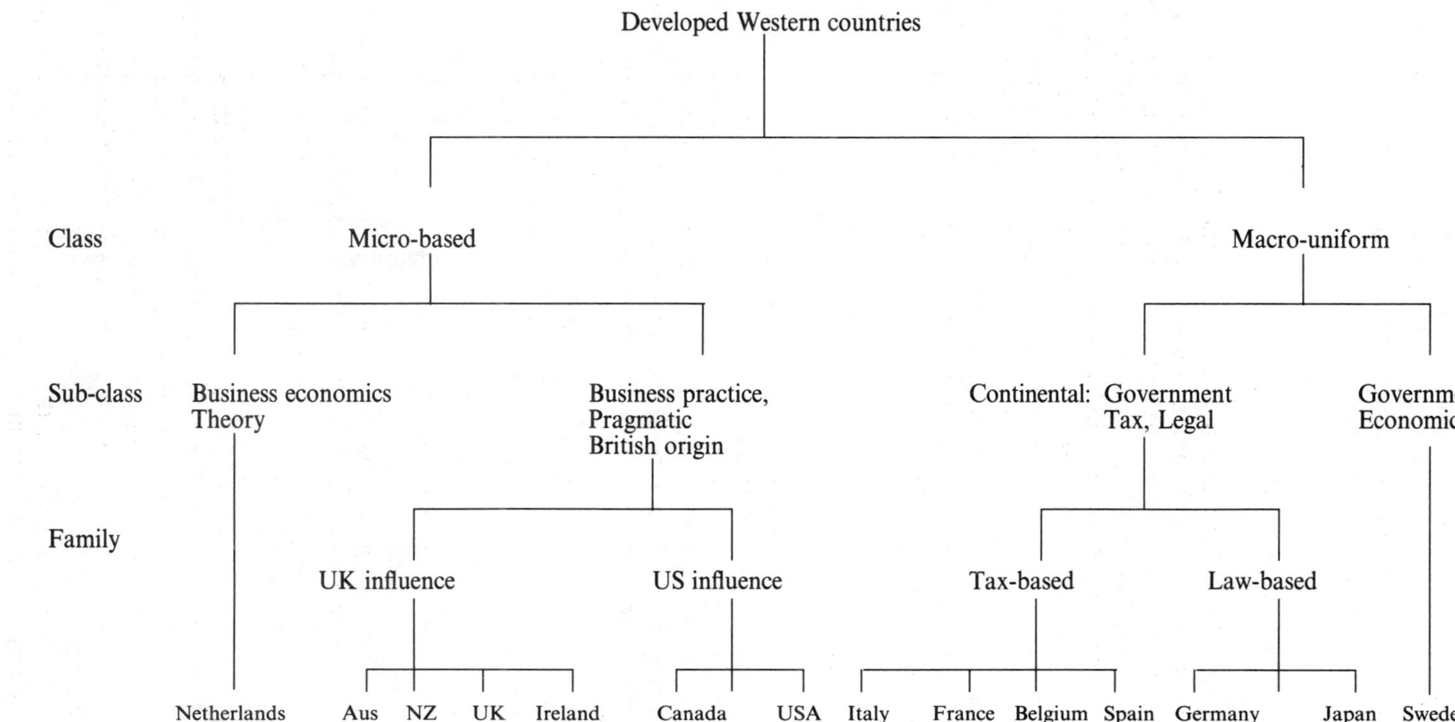

Table 3.3 Classification of Some European Countries

- Measurement Practices
  - Micro / Professional
    - Business Economics
      - Netherlands
    - Pragmatic
      - Denmark
      - UK
      - Ireland
  - Macro / Uniform
    - Code
      - Italy
      - Lux
    - Plan
      - Portugal
      - France
      - Belgium
      - Spain
      - Greece
    - Law (HC)
      - Germany
      - Switzerland
    - Govt Economics
      - Sweden

former involves accountants in individual companies striving to present fair information to outside users, without detailed constraints of law or tax rules but with professional guidelines. The latter type has accounting mainly as a servant of the state, particularly for taxation purposes.

The micro/professional side contains the Netherlands, Denmark, the UK and Ireland (and, outside Europe, it also contains the USA, Australia, New Zealand and Canada). The Netherlands is even more free of rules than are the UK and Ireland, although the influence of micro-economic theory has led to use of replacement cost information to varying degrees.

The macro/uniform side contains all other European countries. However, they can be divided into groups. For example, accounting plans are now the predominant source of detailed rules in France, Belgium, Spain and Greece. In Germany and Switzerland, company law is the major authority, but the former country has much stricter observance of historical cost values and tax-based depreciation. In Italy, Luxembourg and Portugal, tax rules are also a vital determinant of detailed practices. Other rules come from commercial codes rather than from accounting plans or company laws. In Sweden, the predominant influence seems to be the government as economic planner and tax collector.

The purpose of Table 3.3 is to organise countries into groups by similarities of financial reporting measurement practices. This means that a knowledge of one country enables inferences to be drawn about others. The 'distance' between two countries is suggested by how far back up the classification it is necessary to go to reach a common point. This should be useful for those accountants and auditors who have to deal with financial reports from several European countries or who have to work in more than one country.

Such a classification also prompts questions about whether harmonisation is desirable and possible. It is to this subject that we now turn.

3.4 Developments in Classification

The classification suggested in Table 3.2 was proposed in the early 1980s, before much of the programme of EC harmonisation of accounting (discussed in the next chapter). If harmonisation is successful, the classification of European countries will become less clear cut. There is a note on this at the end of the next chapter.

Meanwhile, researchers have been continuing work on classification in order to include more countries and try new methods (eg Al Najjar, 1986; Nobes, 1992).

References

AAA (1977) *Accounting Review, Supplement to Vol 52*, American Accounting Association.

AICPA (1964) *Professional Accounting in 25 Countires*, AICPA, New York.

AICPA (1975) *Professional Accounting in 30 Countries*, AICPA, New York.

Al Najjar, F (1986) 'Standardization in accounting practices: a comparative international study', *International Journal of Accounting*, Spring.

Choi, F D S and Mueller, G G (1984) *International Accounting*, Prentice-Hall, ch 2.

David, R and Brierley, J E C (1978) *Major Legal Systems in the World Today*, Stevens, London.

Hatfield, H R (1966) 'Some variations in accounting practices in England, France, Germany and the US', *Journal of Accounting Research*, Autumn.

Mueller, G G (1967) *International Accounting*, Part I, Macmillan.

Nair, R D and Frank, W G (1980) 'The impact of disclosure and measurement practices on international accounting classifications', *Accounting Review*, July.

Nobes, C W (1983) 'A judgmental international classification of financial reporting practices', *Journal of Business Finance and Accounting*, Spring.

Nobes, C W (1992) *International Classification of Financial Reporting*, Routledge, London.

Price Waterhouse (1973 and 1975) *Accounting Principles and Reporting Practices* ICAEW, London.

Price Waterhouse (1979) *International Survey of Accounting Principles and Reporting Practices*, Butterworth.

Seidler, L J (1966) 'International accounting – the ultimate theory course', *Accounting Review*, October.

Zeff, S A (1972) *Forging Accounting Principles in Five Countries*, Stipes Publishing, Champaign, Illinois.

CHAPTER 4

EC Harmonisation

4.1 Definition

'Harmonisation' is not an easy word to define. Its arrival in common use in the context of accounting and law seems to be associated with the EC. However, neither the Commission nor other organs of the EC have explicitly defined the word. There seem to be two usages. The most frequently occurring meaning is that two or more systems (of accounting practices or corporate taxation, for example) are made to look more like one another. The rather more subtle alternative meaning is that, without necessarily causing approximation, the systems are made compatible. Some differences can be lived with happily and others cannot be. By analogy, in music it is possible to move discordant notes farther apart and yet make them more harmonious. In practice, harmonisation in accounting tends to mean the process of increasing the compatibility of accounting practices by setting bounds to their degree of variation.

The word 'standardisation' might appear to be stronger, implying the process of making things the same rather than compatible. To some extent, this is true for UK accounting standards. In some cases these standards prescribe only one method, and promulgate practice in some detail. However, in many cases, accounting standards merely narrow the range of acceptable practices; this is particularly the case with international standards. Furthermore, whereas the 'harmonisation' proceeding from the EC leads to law, the process of international 'standardisation' encouraged by the International Accounting Standards Committee (IASC) has much less powerful backing (see section 4.8). Thus, in accounting, contrary to the general nuances of the words, 'harmonisation' appears to mean something more strict than 'standardisation'. The words themselves and the difference between them are sufficiently vague that it is proposed here to use them in their normal contexts and without the implication of a precise differentiation between them.

4.2 Reasons for Harmonisation

The preparation and products of accounting information are becoming increasingly international. Multinational groups are becoming more dominant and diversifying ever more widely geographically; the holding of shares across national boundaries by persons and (particularly) by institutions is increasingly common, as illustrated by the listing of a growing number of foreign shares and debentures on the New York and London Exchanges; and the multinational accounting firms are constantly expanding their fields of interest and absorbing indigenous firms. These developments increase the practical importance of the differences between accounting systems.

The preceding chapters have discussed the causes of differences in financial reporting in Europe, the nature of those differences, and the way in which the differences may be grouped together. It is clear that, to compilers and interpreters of financial statements from more than one country, these differences are of great significance for the valuation of assets and the measurement of profits. The reasons that make *national* accounting standards desirable also apply internationally. These reasons include the desire to exclude the use of certain misleading practices and to narrow the range of acceptable alternatives so that accounting figures are more comparable between companies. The need for *international* comparability is obvious where shareholders, bankers or revenue authorities operate across national boundaries. Thus, some of the pressure for harmonisation comes from such users. Again, it is not necessary to make accounting rules identical in all relevant countries, but to ensure that they are at least compatible in the sense that, by using information disclosed, useful international comparisons of financial statements can be achieved.

It is not only the various users who might benefit from harmonisation; the compilers and auditors of published financial statements also stand to gain. Further, the differences in accounting are important not only in the context of published financial statements. Because a company's internal accounting system is often heavily influenced by the need to report to shareholders, to governments or to revenue authorities, international differences are also important internally. Such differences lead to problems of performance measurement and investment appraisal within multinational groups.

In summary, the following groups might gain most from European or wider harmonisation of financial reporting:

(*i*) *Investors, investment analysts and stock exchanges*: to enable international comparisons for investment decisions.
(*ii*) *Credit grantors*: for similar reasons to (*i*).
(*iii*) *Multinational companies*: as compilers, investors, appraisers of products or staff, and as staff circulators.
(*iv*) *Multinational accountancy firms*: as auditors and advisers of companies operating in several countries.
(*v*) *Governments*: as tax collectors and controllers of multinationals.

4.3 Factors against Harmonisation

There is a fundamental argument against harmonisation which has been illustrated by the preceding chapters. That is, to the extent that international differences in accounting practices result from underlying economic, legal, social and other environmental factors, harmonisation may not be justified. Different accounting has grown up to serve the different needs of different users; this might suggest that the existing accounting is the 'correct' form for its habitat and should not be changed merely to simplify the work of multinational companies. There does seem to be strength in this point particularly for smaller companies with no significant multinational activities or connections. To foist upon a small private family company in Luxembourg lavish disclosure requirements and the need to report a 'true and fair' view may not be a sensible piece of harmonisation.

The most obvious obstacle to harmonisation is the sheer size and deep-rootedness of the differences in accounting. Even within the 'micro-accounting' or Anglo-Dutch class of countries (see Chapter 3), there are important differences which are difficult to remove. Nevertheless, these pale into insignificance compared to the differences between this class and German accounting. As has been discussed, these differences have grown up over the previous century because of differences in users, legal systems and so on. Thus, the differences are structural rather than cosmetic, and require revolutionary action to remove them.

Another facet of this is that professional bodies are strong in Anglo-Dutch countries and weak in most continental European countries. This means that it is impossible for professional bodies directly to achieve international harmonisation throughout the developed western world. Thus, although the professional bodies may be able to make some progress in the Anglo-Dutch world, government intervention would be necessary for a wider harmonisation. This brings us to a consideration of the obstacle of nationalism, which may show itself in an unwillingness to accept compromises which involve changing accounting practices towards those of other countries. This unwillingness may be on the part of accountants and companies or on the part of states who may not wish to lose their sovereignty. Another manifestation of nationalism may be the lack of knowledge or interest in accounting elsewhere. A rather more subtle and acceptable variety of this is the concern that it would be difficult to alter internationally set standards in response to a change of mind or a change of circumstances.

Minor difficulties of language are added to by more complex problems like the translation of 'true and fair'. Particularly in the 1970s, there was considerable incomprehension of this expression in France and Germany, which surfaced most clearly at international conferences.

4.4 Directives and Regulations

The EC achieves its harmonising objectives through two main instruments: Directives, which must be incorporated into the laws of member states; and Regulations, which become law throughout the EC without the need to pass through national legislatures. The concern of this chapter will be with the Directives on company law and with two Regulations. These are listed in Table 4.1 overleaf, which also gives a brief description of their scope. The company law Directives of most relevance to accounting are the Fourth and Seventh. These will be discussed in more detail below, after an outline of the procedure for setting Directives.

First, the Commission which is the EC's permanent civil service decides on a project and asks an expert to prepare a report. In the case of the Fourth Directive, this was the Elmendorff Report of 1967. Then an *avant projet* or discussion document is prepared. This is studied by a Commission working party and may lead to the issue of a draft proposed Directive which is commented on by the European Parliament (a directly elected assembly with limited powers) and the Economic and Social Committee (a consultative body of employers, employees and others). A revised proposal is then

Table 4.1 Directives Relevant to Corporate Accounting

Directives on Company Law	**Draft Dates**	**Date Adopted**	**Purpose**	**UK Law**
First	1964	1968	Ultra vires rules	1972
Second	1970, 1972	1976	Separation of public companies, minimum capital, distributions	1980
Third	1970, 1973 1975	1978	Mergers	1987
Fourth	1971, 1974	1978	Formats and rules of accounting	1981
Fifth	1972, 1983		Structure and audit of public companies	
Sixth	1975, 1978	1982	De-mergers	1987
Seventh	1976, 1978	1983	Consolidated accounting	1989
Eighth	1978, 1979	1984	Qualifications and work of auditors	1989
Ninth	—		Links between public company groups	
Tenth	1985		International mergers of public companies	
Eleventh	1986	1989	Disclosures relating to branches	
Twelfth	1988	1989	Single member companies	
Vredeling	1980, 1983		Employee information and consultation	
Regulations				
Societas Europea	1970, 1978, 1989		European company	
European Economic Interest Grouping	1973, 1978	1985	Joint venture structure	

submitted to a Working Party of the Council of Ministers. The Council, consisting of the relevant ministers from each EC country, is the body that adopts a Directive or Regulation. In the case of a Directive, member states are required to introduce a national law within a specified period, though they often exceed it. The Fourth Directive, adopted in June 1978 and notified to member states in July, specified a two-year period followed by up to 18 months for the national law to come into effect. A note on implementation can be found at the end of section 4.6.

Let us take the UK as an example of the enactment of Directives. The First Directive was included in the UK's enabling legislation for entry into the EC in 1972. The requirements of the Second Directive were included in the 1980 Companies Act after many additions concerning insider trading, directors duties and several other matters. The Fourth Directive led to the 1981 Companies Act, again with various additions, such as rules on merger accounting and the purchase of own shares. The Third and Sixth Directives (which concern special types of mergers and de-mergers) were implemented by Statutory Instrument in 1987. The Seventh and Eighth Directives were included in the 1989 Companies Act.

4.5 The Second Directive

Of the various matters dealt with by the Second Directive, perhaps the most obvious are the naming of companies, the minimum capital requirements of public companies, and the definition of distributable profit. The first of these was examined in section 1.2 and Table 1.2. As a result of the Second Directive, the UK and Ireland introduced the designation 'public limited company', and the Netherlands created the BV as the private limited company.

It has been normal in continental Europe for there to be minimum capital requirements for companies. The Second Directive imposes such a requirement for public companies. The 1980 Act introduced a minimum requirement of £50,000 issued share capital for UK public companies. The Directive contained no requirements for private companies, and none has been introduced in the UK. However, in Germany the *GmbH Gesetz* (1980) raised the minimum capital requirement of private companies to DM 50,000.

As for the definition of distributable profit, the Directive introduced a definition which in UK law is expressed as: 'accumulated realised profits ... less ... accumulated realised losses'. Further, the Directive requires that dividends must not be distributed if they would reduce the net assets below the total of capital and undistributable reserves.

4.6 The Fourth Directive

Survey of Contents

Before examining the effects on particular EC countries, the Fourth Directive itself will be discussed. Article 1 states that the Directive relates to public and private companies throughout the EC, except that member states need not apply the provisions to banks, insurance companies and other financial institutions (for whom there are special versions of the Fourth Directive).[1] Article 2 defines the annual accounts to which it refers as the balance sheet, profit and loss account and notes. Reference to funds flow statements which are standard in the UK and other countries is omitted. The accounts 'shall be drawn up clearly and in accordance with the provisions' of the Directive, except that the need to present a 'true and fair view' may require extra information or may demand a departure from the provisions of the Directive. Such departures must be disclosed. The Directive is intended to establish minimum standards and 'member states may authorise or require' extra disclosure.

[1] The bank accounts Directive was adopted in 1986 and the insurance accounts Directive in 1991.

Articles 3 to 7 contain general provisions about the consistency and detail of the formats for financial statements. There is a specified order of items, and some items cannot be combined or omitted. Corresponding figures for the previous year must be shown. Articles 8 to 10 detail two formats for balance sheets, one or both of which may be allowed by member states. The Articles allow some combination and omission of immaterial items, but the outline and much detail will be standard.

Articles 11 and 12 allow member states to permit small companies to publish considerably abridged balance sheets. 'Small companies' are those falling below two of the following limits: balance sheet total, 1 million units of account (UA); turnover, 2 million EC units of account; employees, 50. There is also the possibility of lesser reductions for medium-sized companies (see Arts 27 and 47). These size limits are capable of being raised and this happened in 1984. Articles 13 and 14 concern details of disclosure, particularly contingent liabilities, which were shown in the UK but not in some other countries. Articles 15 to 21 concern the definition and disclosure of assets and liabilities. It is useful that 'value adjustments' must be disclosed (Art 15(3)(a)); this will make clearer the conservative revaluations which are common in Franco-German systems.

Articles 22 to 26 specify four formats for profit and loss accounts, which member states may allow companies to choose between. Two of these classify expenses and revenues by nature, and the other two classify them by stage of production. There are two in each case because vertical or two-sided versions may be chosen. Compared with the former sparse UK profit and loss accounts, the disclosure of expenses became very detailed.

However, Art 27 allows member states to permit medium-sized companies to avoid disclosure of the items making up gross profit. In this case original limits were: balance sheet total, 4 million UA; turnover, 8 million UA; employees, 250. Articles 28 to 30 contain some definitions relating to the profit and loss accounts.

Articles 31 and 32 lay out general rules of valuation. The normal Anglo-Dutch principles of accounting are promulgated. Article 33 is a fairly lengthy explanation of the Directive's stance towards accounting for inflation or for specific price changes. Whatever happens, member states must ensure that historical cost information is either shown or can be calculated using notes to the accounts. However, member states may permit or require supplementary or main accounts to be prepared on a replacement value, current purchasing power or other basis. Revaluation of assets would entail a balancing Revaluation Reserve; there are detailed requirements relating to this.

Articles 34 to 42 relate to detailed valuation and disclosure requirements for various balance sheet items. Again the point about the disclosure of 'exceptional value adjustments' is made, this time with specific reference to taxation-induced writings down (Arts 35(1)(d) and 39(e)). The periods over which research and development expenditure and goodwill are written off are to be standardised (Art 37).

Articles 43 to 46 concern the large number of disclosures which will be obligatory in the annual report, including the notes to the accounts. In general, these were already provided in the UK. 'Small companies' (as in Art 11) may be partially exempted. Articles 47 to 51 relate to the audit and publication of accounts. In general, procedures for these matters were allowed to remain as they had been under different national laws. Member states may exempt 'small companies' from publishing profit and loss accounts (Art 47(2)(b)) and from audit (Art 51). This would mean that they would only produce unaudited abridged balance sheets. Article 47(3) allows member states to permit 'medium-sized companies' (as in Art 27) to abridge their balance sheets and notes. However, this abridgement is not as extensive as that for 'small companies', and audit and profit and loss accounts are necessary.

Articles 52 to 62 deal with the implementation of the Directive and with transitional problems, particularly those relating to consolidation, which await the Seventh Directive. A 'Contact Committee' is to be set up to facilitate the application of the Directive and to advise on amendments or additions. Article 55 calls for member states to pass the necessary laws within two years of the July 1978 notification, and then to bring these into force within a further 18 months.

Commentary

The Directive's articles include those referring to valuation rules, formats of published financial statements and disclosure requirements. However, the Directive does not cover the process of consolidation, which is left for the Seventh Directive. As has been mentioned, the EC Commission entrusted the task of preparing the *avant projet* for the Fourth Directive to a working party chaired by a German, Dr. Elmendorff. It is not surprising, then, that the first draft of the Directive, published in 1971 (as Table 4.1 records), was based substantially on the German *Aktiengesetz* (Public Companies Act) of 1965. This draft was published before the UK and Ireland entered the EC.

The Directive deals with annual balance sheets and profit and loss accounts, but not with supplementary statements like funds flow statements. The contents of the Directive are discussed below under four headings.

1 Formats

Compared with traditional Anglo-Dutch accounting, perhaps the most obvious feature of the *Aktiengesetz* (*AktG*), and thus of the Fourth Directive, is the prescription of uniform formats. The *AktG*, which was the law for German public companies until 1987 year ends, offered no choice between formats, nor any substantial flexibility within a format. As might have been expected, there was considerable difficulty in arriving at agreed formats for the first draft of the Fourth Directive, even among the six member states belonging to the EC in 1971. This shows itself in the inclusion in the Directive of two balance sheet formats and four profit and loss account formats. These remained largely unaltered in the second draft and the final Directive.

Looking first at the balance sheet, the original German format was reproduced with slight amendment in the 1971 draft of the Fourth Directive (see Table 4.2 opposite). This is a two-sided (or horizontal) balance sheet, with assets on the left. The only significant change between the 1971 draft and those of 1974 and 1978 is in the classification of reserves. The *AktG* and the 1971 draft Directive show profits as the last item on the *credit* side of the balance sheet, and losses as the last item on the *debit* side. Such a treatment of profits fits better with a creditors' or entity view rather than a proprietors' view.

Table 4.2 The Evolution of the Balance Sheet (abbreviated versions)

ASSETS shown on left

	AktG (S 151)		**1971 Draft (AA 8)**		**1981 Act (Format 2)**
I	Unpaid capital	A	Unpaid capital	A	Unpaid capital
		B	Formation expenses		
II	Fixed and financial	C	Fixed assets	B	Fixed assets
	A Fixed & intangible		I Intangible		I Intangible
			II Tangible		II Tangible
	B Financial		III Participations		III Investments
III	Current assets	D	Current assets	C	Current assets
	A Stocks		I Stocks		I Stocks
	B Other current		II Debtors		II Debtors
			III Securities		III Investments
					IV Cash
IV	Deferred charges	E	Prepayments	D	Prepayments
V	Accumulated losses	F	Loss		
			I For the year		
			II Brought forward		

LIABILITIES AND CAPITAL shown on right

I	Share capital	A	Subscribed capital	A	Capital & reserves
II	Disclosed reserves	B	Reserves		I Called up capital
III	Provisions for diminutions	C	Value adjustments		II Share premium
					III Revaluation reserves
					IV Other reserves
					V Profit and loss
IV	Provisions for liabilities	D	Provisions for charges	B	Provisions for L & C
V	Liabilities (4 years +)	E	Creditors	C	Creditors
VI	Other liabilities				
VII	Deferred income	F	Accruals	D	Accruals
VIII	Profit	G	Profit		
			I For the year		
			II Brought forward		

However, in the final Directive, a more Anglo-Dutch approach to reserves is adopted. Format 2 of the 1981 Act (see Table 4.2) follows that of the Directive, except for permitted deletions like formation expenses, which was a necessary heading for practice in some countries. Table 4.2 illustrates the gradual and slight changes in the formats over the 16-year period. It shows only the first two levels of headings. A third level (of sub-sub-headings) is omitted, but in each case does exist and is preceded by Arabic numbers.

Chapter 5 examines the present formats used in several European countries. There it may be seen that harmonisation has not led all balance sheets throughout the EC to look like an expanded version of the format in Table 4.2. There are several reasons why this is not the case. First, the Directive contains another format, as discussed in Chapter 5. Member states were allowed to adopt one format or to permit companies to make the choice as long as they are consistent. The UK and Dutch Acts do the latter, and present the vertical forms as 'Format 1' and 'Format A' respectively, presumably on the grounds that this format corresponds much more closely with previous UK and Dutch practice for published accounts (at least those of large companies). However, the French[2] revised *plan comptable* and the German law allow only the horizontal format. The vertical format contains broadly the same headings, sub-headings and sub-sub-headings as the horizontal format, except that current liabilities are shown separately and positioned so as to enable a calculation of net current assets and then net assets.

Secondly, there are several ways in which flexibility is allowed. The *AktG* permitted (i) different classifications for particular trades, (ii) extra detail to be added, and (iii) empty headings to be omitted. The Directive contains these provisions, and also allows Arabic number headings to be combined where the amounts are separately immaterial or where this would lead to greater clarity (in this latter case the information must be shown by note).

Thirdly, more flexibility exists within the Directive's formats than in the *AktG*. This takes the form of several alternative presentations of particular items.

Turning now to the profit and loss account, there is one format only in the *AktG*, but four in each of the versions of the Directive. Member states are allowed to impose particular formats or to allow companies to choose between them. Chapter 5 illustrates how this has been done for some EC countries.

2 *Publication and Audit Exemptions*

It had long been the practice in many EC countries to exempt all private companies (or small ones) from publication or audit requirements or both. The Directive allows various exemptions for small and medium-sized private companies. Member states may exempt small private companies from drawing up full accounts and from publication of the profit and loss account and from audit. Medium-sized companies may be allowed to draw up abridged profit and loss accounts and not to disclose certain notes. The size criteria and the exemptions adopted in some EC countries are examined in Chapter 5.

3 *Accounting 'Principles'*

Anglo-Dutch financial reporting has traditionally been free of legal constraints in the area of principles of valuation and measurement, whether from company law, tax law or accounting plan. However, this is far from the case in some other EC countries, especially Germany whose *Aktiengesetz* was a

[2] For French group accounts, the 1985 revisions to the *plan comptable* allows the full range of formats.

major source of the Fourth Directive. There are three levels of principle in the *AktG*, in the Directive and in the resulting laws of member states. The first and 'vaguest' level consists of a statement of the overriding purpose of the financial statements. In the *AktG* this was the provisions of the law. By the final 1978 version of the Directive, the overriding purpose had become to give a true and fair view. The evolution of this may be seen in Table 4.3. Pressure from the UK, Ireland and the Netherlands had caused its insertion in the 1974 draft and its dominance in the Directive 'in special circumstances'. It should be noted that neither the concept nor the special circumstances need be defined.

The second level of principles has also been substantially affected by Anglo-Dutch accounting. Four accounting conventions found in a British accounting standard, SSAP 2, are enshrined in Art 31 of the Directive: going concern, consistency, prudence and accruals. The first and the last were missing from the first draft of the Directive. However, a fifth principle has been taken from German law, that is the principle that assets and liabilities should be valued separately (for example, when using the lower of cost and net realisable value) before being added together. The concepts were fundamentally acceptable to the Anglo-Dutch view but it was of course a fundamental change of philosophy to find fairly detailed accounting concepts imposed by statute. This change clearly results from the *AktG*.

The third level of principles is more detailed, and, for the UK, Ireland and the Netherlands, involves further encroachment of statute into territory previously regarded as that of the profession. Here, the influence of the *AktG* on the Directive is again clear. In order to enable comparisons within and between industries, to perform meaningful aggregations of companies' accounting figures, and to control the economy, it has seemed appropriate to several continental countries not just to establish uniform formats but to ensure that the items within them are uniformly valued and measured.

The following rules are found in the *AktG* and the Directive:

(*i*) Fixed assets shall be carried at purchase price or construction cost.
(*ii*) Intangibles may only be shown as assets if acquired for valuable consideration.
(*iii*) Fixed assets with limited useful lives must be depreciated.
(*iv*) The basic rule for valuing current assets is 'lower of cost or net realisable value'.
(*v*) Current asset valuation may use FIFO, AVCO, LIFO, or similar method.

As with the concepts discussed above, the content of these rules is not out of character for Anglo-Dutch accounting, but their statutory nature was a fundamental change. This has led to several difficulties between law and standards.

Finally, provisions in the Directive allow alternative rules to a strict Germanic historical cost. Departures from historical cost are allowed, ranging from *ad hoc* revaluations of fixed assets to full scale current cost accounting as statutory accounts. Even the first draft of the Directive (before British entry to the EC) allowed for such departures, which would have been necessary to allow for the practice of many Dutch companies. However, the effect is clearly to destroy the attempt to establish uniform accounting measurement rules. Nevertheless, there are important penalties for adopting

Table 4.3 'True and Fair' in the Fourth Directive

1965 Aktiengesetz (S 149)

1 The annual financial statements shall conform to proper accounting principles. They shall be clear and well set out and give as sure a view of the company's financial position and its operating results as is possible pursuant to the valuation provisions.

1971 Draft (Art 2)

1 The annual accounts shall comprise the balance sheet, the profit and loss account and the notes on the accounts. These documents shall constitute a composite whole.

2 The annual accounts shall conform to the principles of regular and proper accounting.

3 They shall be drawn up clearly and, in the context of the provisions regarding the valuation of assets and liabilities and the lay-out of accounts, shall reflect as accurately as possible the company's assets, liabilities, financial position and results.

1974 Draft (Art 2)

1 (As 1971 Draft).

2 The annual accounts shall give a true and fair view of the company's assets, liabilities, financial position and results.

3 They shall be drawn up clearly and in conformity with the provisions of this Directive.

1978 Final (Art 2)

1 (As 1971 Draft).

2 They shall be drawn up clearly and in accordance with the provisions of this Directive.

3 The annual accounts shall give a true and fair view of the company's assets, liabilities, financial position and profit or loss.

4 Where the application of the provisions of this Directive would not be sufficient to give a true and fair view within the meaning of paragraph 3, additional information must be given.

5 Where in exceptional cases the application of a provision of this Directive is incompatible with the obligation laid down in paragraph 3, that provision must be departed from in order to give a true and fair view within the meaning of paragraph 3. Any such departure must be disclosed in the notes on the accounts together with an explanation of the reasons for it and a statement of its effect on the assets, liabilities, financial position and profit or loss. The member states may define the exceptional cases in question and lay down the relevant special rules.

6 The member states may authorise or require the disclosures in the annual accounts of other information as well as that which must be disclosed in accordance with this Directive.

(or having previously adopted) an alternative to 'Germanic accounting' for any item. These take the form of disclosure requirements, for example in the UK there must be notes concerning:

(*i*) the valuation basis used,
(*ii*) the comparable historical cost amount or the difference,
(*iii*) the comparable accumulated depreciation under historical cost or the difference,
(*iv*) the revaluation reserve relating to all departures,
(*v*) a note of valuation revisions due to adoption of alternative methods in the year,
(*vi*) the year of valuation,
(*vii*) for assets revalued in the year, the names or qualifications of the valuers.

4 Disclosure Requirements

Disclosure rules are a normal part of any country's statutory requirements. The Fourth Directive includes a large number. Many may be traced to the *AktG* but there are others, such as the requirement to show any effects of tax requirements on accounting numbers, that are an attempt to ensure the provision of information acceptable to those used to Anglo-Dutch accounting.

In several EC countries which had very limited disclosure requirements, the Directive involves major changes.

Implementation

As was mentioned earlier, the Fourth Directive was supposed to be implemented by 1980 and to be in force by 1982. This schedule was not achieved by any country. The dates of implementation are shown in Table 4.4 below. The dates on which the provisions came into force were, of course, after the dates in Table 4.4. For example, the German law of 1985 was generally to be complied with by 31.12.1987 year-ends for Fourth Directive elements; 1984 year-ends for France; 1990 for Spain; 1993 for Italy.

4.7 The Seventh Directive

This section considers the contents of the Seventh Directive on group accounts. With the Fourth, this is the other major Directive on financial reporting. Drafts of the Directive were published in 1976 and 1978, and the Directive was adopted in 1983. The fact that a Directive on group accounting was adopted as a separate and later Directive from the Fourth is a reminder of the traditional differences in consolidation practices within the EC. British and Dutch accountants might have expected that this issue, which is central for many sets of statutory accounts, would have figured prominently in the EC Commission's plans for rules on financial reporting. Its absence may be explained by the rarity of consolidation in EC member states in the early 1970s. This is discussed in Chapter 2.

Table 4.4 Implementation of Directives*

	Fourth	**Seventh**
Belgium	1985	1990
Denmark	1981	1990
France	1983	1985
Germany	1985	1985
Greece	1986	1987
Luxembourg	1984	1988
Ireland	1986	1992
Italy	1991	1991
Netherlands	1983	1988
Portugal	1989	1991
Spain	1989	1989
UK	1981	1989

*These are the dates of the laws; in many cases there is a considerable delay before they are brought into force.

The later drafting of the Seventh Directive (subsequent to the accession of the UK, Ireland and Denmark to the EC) helps to explain its Anglo-Dutch, shareholder orientation. The predominance of the Anglo-Dutch view in the 1976 and 1978 drafts became even more noticeable in the adopted Directive of 1983.

Review of Contents

Articles 1–4 require undertakings (which member states may restrict to mean limited companies) to draw up consolidated accounts which include subsidiaries and sub-subsidiaries etc, irrespective of their location. Subsidiaries are defined with respect to majority voting rights or appointment of board members, or dominant influence by contract (these might be called *de jure* criteria). However, member states may also require consolidation of companies managed on a unified basis and companies over which a dominant influence is exercised (*de facto* criteria).

Article 5 allows member states to exempt financial holding companies that do not manage their subsidiaries or take part in board appointments. Article 6 allows member states to exempt medium sized and small groups, using the criteria of the Fourth Directive (see Chapter 5) and assuming that no listed company is included. However, until the year 2000, member states may use larger size criteria as specified.

Articles 7 to 11 exempt a company from the requirement to consolidate its own subsidiaries if it is itself a wholly owned subsidiary of an EC company (or a 90% or more owned subsidiary whose minority shareholders approve). However, member states may insist on consolidation by listed subsidiaries. On the other hand, member states may also allow other (less fully owned) subsidiaries not to consolidate unless a certain proportion of shareholders require it. Exemption from consolidation may be linked to a requirement to produce extra information, and the exemption does not necessarily extend to employee reports. Also, member states may exempt further subsidiaries if they are themselves subsidiaries of non-EC parents that prepare suitable consolidated accounts.

Article 12 allows member states to require consolidation where companies are managed on a unified basis or are managed by the same persons.

Articles 13 to 15 allow various subsidiaries to be excluded from consolidation if they are immaterial, if there is severe long-term restriction on assets or management, if there would be disproportionate expense or delay, if they are held for resale, or if their activities are dissimilar (these latter must be excluded if they threaten the true and fair view).

Article 16 requires that consolidated accounts shall be clear and shall give a true and fair view. Article 17 requires the Fourth Directive's formats to be used, suitably amended. Article 18 requires consolidation to be 100%. Article 19 requires there to be a once-and-for-all calculation of goodwill based on fair values at the date of first consolidation or at the date of purchase.

Article 20 allows merger accounting where any cash payment represents less than 10% of the nominal value of the shares issued. Articles 21–23 require minority interests to be shown separately, and 100% of income of consolidated companies to be included. Articles 24–28 require consistency, elimination of intra-group items, use of the parent's year-end as the group's year-end (normally), and disclosure of information to enable meaningful temporal comparisons where the composition of the group has changed.

Article 29 requires the valuation rules of the Fourth Directive to be used, and uniform rules to be used for the consolidation of all subsidiaries. There must be disclosure of differences between parent and group practices. Tax-based valuations must be 'corrected' (or member states may allow them merely to be disclosed) in the consolidation.

Articles 30–31 require positive goodwill on consolidation to be depreciated or to be immediately written off against reserves, and negative goodwill only to be taken to profit if it is realised or where it was due to the expectation of future costs or losses.

Article 32 allows member states to require or permit proportional consolidation for joint ventures. Article 33 requires associated companies to be recorded as a single item, initially valued at cost or at the proportion of net assets. Subsequently, the appropriate share of profits must be included in the group accounts.

Articles 34 to 36 call for a large number of disclosures relating to group companies and consolidation methods. Articles 37 and 38 deal with publication and audit. Articles 39 to 51 deal with transitional and enabling provisions.

Commentary

The 1976 and 1978 drafts of the Directive contained many more elements of continental European practice than does the adopted version described above. For example, *de facto* rather than *de jure* control was the criterion for consolidation; consolidation was required even where the head of the group was not a company; and EC level consolidations ('horizontal consolidations') were required when the head of the company was registered outside the EC. These three ideas remain in the Directive but they are now options.

The resulting Directive is very close to UK practice in its main provisions.

As an illustration of this, some main provisions are listed in Table 4.5 below, showing which countries' pre-Directive practices they accord closest with. In addition, some of the options are examined in the same way in Table 4.6 overleaf.

Clearly great changes were or are in store for countries other than the UK, Ireland and the Netherlands. The most noticeable changes in Germany are the extension of consolidation to more groups, the inclusion of associated companies and foreign subsidiaries, and a new method of calculating differences arising on consolidation. In France, the most obvious changes are extension of the rules beyond listed companies and the imposition of greater uniformity. In Italy, Greece, Portugal, Spain and Luxembourg consolidation will cease to be a great rarity.

Implementation

The Seventh Directive was intended to be implemented throughout the EC by 1 January 1988 (except for delays allowed for Greece, Spain and Portugal). Although France and Germany were slow to enact the Fourth Directive, they have been the leaders with the Seventh: in January 1985 (partially) and in December 1985, respectively. Implementation dates are shown in Table 4.4.

Many options still remain in the Directive and, at the time of writing, several countries have not decided precisely how to implement it. Chapter 8 examines the consolidation practice of several European countries in more detail. As an example of differences, Table 8.3 shows the implementation (or proposed implementation) of certain aspects of the definition of a subsidiary.

Table 4.5 Main Provisions of Seventh Directive

		Source Countries
Art 1	Subsidiaries defined principally in terms of *de jure* criteria	UK, IRL
Art 3	Consolidation to include foreign subsidiaries	UK, IRL, NL, F
Art 4	Consolidation irrespective of legal form of subsidiary	G
Art 4	Consolidation by all types of companies	UK, IRL, NL
Art 7	Exemption from preparation of group accounts by wholly-owned subsidiaries	UK, IRL, NL, F
Art 13	Exclusion on basis of immateriality, long-term restrictions, expense or delay	UK, IRL, NL, F
Art 16	True and fair view	UK, IRL, NL
Art 17	Uniform formats to be used	G, F
Art 19	Goodwill to be calculated once-for-all	UK, IRL, NL, F
Art 19	Goodwill to be based on fair values	UK, IRL, NL
Art 29	Tax-based valuations to be 'corrected' or at least disclosed	UK, IRL, NL
Art 30	Goodwill to be depreciated or written off	UK, IRL, NL, F
Art 33	Equity method for associated companies	UK, IRL, NL, F

Table 4.6 Options in the Seventh Directive

		Source Countries
Arts 1, 12	Group companies to include those managed on a unified basis or dominantly influenced	NL, G
Art 4	Requirements to consolidate may be restricted to parents that are companies	UK, IRL
Art 5	Financial holding companies may be exempted	Lux
Art 6	Consolidation may be restricted to 'large' groups	approx F, G
Art 11	Groups exempted if owned by non-EC parents that prepare suitable accounts	UK, IRL, NL
Art 20	Merger accounting allowed	UK
Art 32	Proportional consolidation allowed	F, NL

4.8 Europe and the IASC

The International Accounting Standards Committee, founded in 1973 after a conference in Sydney, is based in London, operates through professional accounting bodies, and works in English. From this it may be seen to be a 'left-hand' country in terms of the classifications of chapter 3. By contrast, EC harmonisation is clearly a 'right-hand' procedure as it operates through laws and is based in Brussels.

Although the IASC might seem very Anglo-Saxon, many of its permanent board members are European (see Table 4.7). Of the 14 board members in 1994, six out of 13 countries were European, as were half of the representatives of the analysts. So, the board is fairly well balanced between European and non-European and between 'left' and 'right'.

The influence of the IASC in Europe can be seen in several ways:

(*i*) *Direct effects on practices.* In some countries, many large companies use international standards (IASs) where there are no domestic rules. This might be the case for currency translation or for certain aspects of consolidation techniques. This use of IASs can be seen in France, Italy

Table 4.7 IASC Board Members (1994)

Australia*	Jordan
Canada*	Netherlands*
France*	Nordic Federation
Germany*	South Africa*
India	UK*
Italy*	US*
Japan*	International Committee of Analysts

* Founder/Permanent members

and Switzerland. In some countries, some listed companies prepare IAS accounts for foreign listings (eg Switzerland).

(*ii*) *Indirect effects on rules.* Rule makers in several European countries are affected by IASs and consider them when drafting domestic rules. This is clearly the case in the UK, France, the Netherlands and Scandinavia.

(*iii*) *Indirect effects on the EC.* In the discussions in Brussels over the years, perhaps particularly those on the Seventh Directive, the existence of IASs agreed by many European representatives would have been persuasive.

4.9 Harmonisation in the 1990s

Although the implementation of the Directives stretched into the 1990s for several countries, few significant accounting measures have been announced by the EC in this decade. There is general agreement that Directives are slow to implement and that they are difficult to change as circumstances change. In 1990, the EC Commission announced that no more accounting Directives would be forthcoming. An EC Forum of standard setters was set up but this seems to have no clear purpose and no power.

It is clear that major harmonisation has been achieved in certain fields. For example, reasonably similar consolidation practices have been spread across the EC; disclosures have been increased in many countries; the variety of formats has been reduced; and independent audit has spread. In 'left-hand' countries, the law has become a major source of accounting rules. In certain 'right-hand' countries, notably France, there has been a major move towards substance/fairness in accounting, particularly for group accounts. This has made the classifications of Chapter 3 less clear cut.

A further aspect of European harmonisation in the 1990s has been the approximate implementation of the Fourth and Seventh Directives in Switzerland and Austria, and the drafting of laws in Sweden and Norway, and in Poland and other eastern countries, influenced by the Directives. This is part of a process of preparing for the expansion of the EC.

A major influence on harmonisation for a few very large listed companies is the need to raise finance on international markets. Such markets operate with large quantities of audited, frequent financial information. In other words, they are 'left-hand' in style. Consequently, many French, Swedish and Swiss companies prepare Anglo-American style annual reports. The process has even begun to affect Germany: in 1993 Daimler-Benz was the first German company to arrange with the US SEC to satisfy the latter's accounting rules for a US listing.

CHAPTER 5

Publication and Audit of Accounts

5.1 Introduction

Because of the importance of 'outsiders' as providers of finance in the UK, Ireland and the Netherlands, there has been a long tradition of voluntary publication and audit of annual accounts. This has been increasingly overtaken in the second half of the twentieth century by the appearance of guidelines or standards from the accountancy profession and of company laws. At one extreme, the UK has required publication and audit for all active limited companies (nearly a million). At the other extreme, publication and audit has been rare in Switzerland and most Mediterranean countries. Even in Germany, until the late 1980s, publication and audit was restricted to a few thousand large and public companies.

As has been discussed in the previous chapter, the EC Fourth Directive allows member states to exempt small companies from audit and from the publication of profit and loss accounts. Some exemptions are also allowed for medium-sized companies. The size definitions are expressed in the Fourth Directive in European currency units (ecu), above which member states may not go. Some examples of member state interpretations of this are shown in Table 5.1 opposite. A company must fall below two of the three thresholds in order to qualify.

Because there are options in the Directive and because member states can always be more severe than the Directive requires, the national laws are different. For example, the UK does not exempt small companies from audit, whereas Germany does. Although the Directive should have led to a massive extension of audit for Germany, most companies are still exempted because most companies are 'small'. Many of those GmbHs which should have been covered by the new requirements changed themselves into a form of limited partnership (GmbH and Co KG) to escape the rules. Others merely failed to comply. Table 5.2 summarises some of the provisions for the four countries.

The amount of supplementary information also differs throughout Europe. Table 5.3 shows some examples for several countries.

5.2 Formats

Uniform formats are originally a German idea, but one now adopted elsewhere; for example, through the accounting plans of France, Spain and Greece. As discussed in the previous chapter, the Fourth Directive imposes

Table 5.1 Size Criteria in Four European Countries

For small companies:

	UK	Netherlands
Turnover:	£2.8 million	fl 10 million
Balance sheet total:	£1.4 million	fl 5 million
Employees:	50	50
	France	**Germany**
Turnover:	FF 3 million	DM 8 million
Balance sheet total:	FF 1.5 million	DM 3.9 million
Employees:	10	50

For medium-sized companies:

	UK	Netherlands
Turnover:	£11.2 million	fl 40 million
Balance sheet total:	£5.6 million	fl 20 million
Employees:	250	250
	France	**Germany**
Turnover:	FF 20 million	DM 32 million
Balance sheet total:	FF 10 million	DM 15.5 million
Employees:	50	250

Table 5.2 Exemptions in Four European Countries

The exemptions from publication and audit are as follows for small companies:

UK	Netherlands
Exemption from publication (though not from audit and sending to shareholders) of profit and loss account, directors' report and many notes; and balance sheet abbreviated.	Abbreviated formats for statements. Also, exempt from audit, and from publication of profit and loss account and directors' report.
France	**Germany**
Abridged accounts and notes may be published. Exempt from audit.	Exempt from audit, and from publication of profit and loss account and directors' report.

For medium-sized companies:

UK	Netherlands
Abbreviated profit and loss account (for publication purposes only).	Abbreviated profit and loss account.
France	**Germany**
Abridged notes in published accounts.	May be audited by Vereidigte Buchprüfer rather than by Wirtschaftsprüfer.

uniform formats, but with some flexibility. Table 5.4 opposite shows how some member states have chosen formats. For France there is greater flexibility than shown here in the case of group accounts. The 'gross profit' and 'total

Table 5.3 Disclosures and Reports

	Cash Flow Statements	Earnings per Share Disclosed	Interim Reports
UK	Required, except for small private companies and wholly owned subsidiaries.	Required for listed companies.	Half-yearly for listed companies.
Netherlands	Majority practice for large companies, but not required and not uniform.	Normal for listed companies, but not required.	Half-yearly for listed companies but vague requirements.
France	Normal for listed companies.	Normal for listed companies, but not required.	Half-yearly for listed companies. Sales required quarterly.
Germany	Not required, therefore no rules, but fairly common for listed companies.	Shown by some listed companies.	Half-yearly required for listed companies from 1989.
Sweden	Required for large companies.	Normal for listed companies, but not required.	Half-yearly required by large companies.
Italy	Required for listed companies.	Uncommon.	Half-yearly reports for listed companies.
Spain	Required by law.	Uncommon.	Quarterly reports by listed companies.

Table 5.4 Format Types in Four European Countries

	UK	**Netherlands**
Balance sheet:	Both allowed. Vertical normal.	Both allowed. Two-sided normal.
Profit & loss:	All allowed. Vertical normal. 'Gross profit' most usual.	All allowed. Vertical normal. 'Gross profit' most usual.
	France	**Germany**
Balance sheet:	Two-sided only.	Two-sided only.
Profit & loss:	'Total output' formats only.	Vertical only. 'Total output' normal.

output' versions of the profit and loss account can be seen in the Appendix to this chapter, for example, in the UK formats 1 and 2. The German company's format in Table 2.1 is a 'total output' version.

5.3 Terminology

Naturally, language can be a major difficulty when dealing with European financial statements. Not only must the analyst master technical accounting terms but foreign languages also. Many large continental European companies publish versions of their accounts in English (or 'American'). However, many do not.

Even accounts in English may have unreliable or misleading translations and, at worst, the English version may be little more than a marketing document. Such versions are, of course, not the real statutory accounts, nor do they have to obey UK rules, so they may be extracts or manipulations of the original.

Some examples of translation problems will help to illustrate these points. The accounts of Total Oil (for France) and AEG (for Germany) are used for this purpose. Full versions of the accounts of these companies can be found in appendices at the end of this book. There is no suggestion that these companies are worse than any others, indeed they are better than many; it is merely that language is a complex problem in a technical area like accounting.

> Example 1 (from 1991)
> The following is an extract from the English-version annual report of Total Oil: 'Foreign currency balance sheets are converted into French francs on the basis of exchange rates at 31 December 1991. The conversion is applied to fixed assets as well as to monetary assets and liabilities. Gains or losses on translation of their balance sheets at the end of the previous year are dealt with . . .'

This extract shows the word 'conversion' being used interchangeably with

*Table 5.5 Illustration of Language Problems**

Original	Author's Interpretation
Capital consolidation is performed using the 'book value method'. Under this method, the book values of the affiliated companies are netted against the underlying equity in these companies at the time of acquisition or initial consolidation. Arising differences are allocated to the book values of assets and liabilities of the affiliates, in so far as their market values of acquisition or initial consolidation deviate from the book values. Remaining positive or negative differences are netted and shown either as goodwill or disclosed as a reduction from reserves.	Full consolidation is performed using a version of fair value accounting. Under this method, the first stage is to compare the cost of the consolidated companies with the book value of the group's share of their net assets. Generally this is done at the date of acquisition, but for existing subsidiaries that have been consolidated for the first time this year, the year end values are used. Where cost exceeds net assets, the difference is allocated to the subsidiary's assets and liabilities up to and in proportion to their fair values. Any excess remaining is goodwill, which is either shown as an asset or written off against reserves. Where the initial exercise leads to a negative difference, this is shown as a 'reserve arising from consolidation'.

*The original is from AEG's published translation of its 1988 Accounts.

'translation' because the two accounting terms are the same in French (*conversion*). In English the former means a physical act of exchange, whereas the latter (which would be correct here) means an accounting manipulation.

Example 2
A further extract, as found in earlier years of Total Oil reports:
'However, as concerns newly acquired companies the excess of the TOTAL Group's investment in such companies ... is capitalized in the consolidated balance sheet and is not amortized. ... These surplus values are depreciated on a straightline basis . . .'

The expression 'surplus values' is a translation of *survaleurs*. The English accounting expression would have been 'goodwill'.

Example 3
When matters get complicated, a translation often becomes opaque. AEG's note on consolidated techniques is very difficult to understand. It is shown in Table

5.5 with the present author's interpretation. The technical points are discussed further in Chapter 8. The version of this method is described somewhat more clearly by Daimler-Benz (see Appendix II).

The general problem illustrated by these examples is that, although the language may be of good quality, the translation is often not done by accountants, perhaps because bilingual accountants are very expensive to hire. For example, there are no such terms in British accounting as 'surplus values' (Example 2) or 'capital consolidation' or 'book value method' (Example 3). Of course, none of this should be read as implying a lack of gratitude for translations: it is a very rare US or UK company that bothers at all.

In order to help the reader as far as possible in cases where there is no translation, there is a four-language glossary of terms at the end of this book. An Anglo-American comparison and a detailed explanation of terms can be found in the companion volume, *Interpreting US Financial Statements*.

Appendix to Chapter 5: Formats

The compulsory or the most frequently found formats for financial statements are shown in the following pages. The lowest level of detail in the formats may generally be disclosed in the notes, so that published accounts do not look exactly as shown in this appendix.

The formats shown here are, in order of appearance:

1 **UK.** The vertical balance sheet used by the great majority of companies.

2 **UK.** The most frequently used profit and loss account.

3 **UK.** The minority-used profit and loss account.

4 **Netherlands.** The vertical balance sheet used by many large companies.

5, 6 **Netherlands.** The two most used profit and loss account formats.

7 **France.** The balance sheet (for individual companies).

8 **France.** The two-sided profit and loss account.

9 **Germany.** The balance sheet.

10 **Germany.** The more normal profit and loss account.

11 **Germany.** The optional profit and loss account.

1

UK, Balance Sheet, Format 1 (presented vertically)

Called up share capital not paid

Fixed assets

Intangible assets
- Development costs
- Concessions, patents, licences, trade marks and similar rights and assets
- Goodwill
- Payments on account

Tangible assets
- Land and buildings
- Plant and machinery
- Fixtures, fittings, tools and equipment
- Payments on account and assets in course of construction

Investments
- Shares in group undertakings
- Loans to group undertakings
- Interests in associated undertakings
- Other participating interests
- Other investments other than loans
- Other loans
- Own shares

Current assets

Stocks
- Raw materials and consumables
- Work in progress
- Finished goods and goods for resale
- Payments on account

Debtors
- Trade debtors
- Amounts owed by group undertakings
- Amounts owed by participating interests
- Other debtors
- Called up share capital not paid
- Prepayments and accrued income

Investments
- Shares in group undertakings
- Own shares
- Other investments

Cash at bank and in hand

Prepayments and accrued income

Creditors: amounts falling due within one year
- Debenture loans
- Bank loans and overdrafts
- Payments received on account
- Trade creditors
- Bills of exchange payable
- Amounts owed to group undertakings
- Amounts owed to participating interests
- Other creditors including taxation and social security
- Accruals and deferred income

Net current assets (liabilities)

Total assets less current liabilities

Creditors: amounts falling due after more than one year

Debenture loans
- Bank loans and overdrafts
- Payments received on account
- Trade creditors
- Bills of exchange payable
- Amounts owed to group undertakings
- Amounts owed to participating interests
- Other creditors including taxation and social security
- Accruals and deferred income

Provisions for liabilities and charges
- Pensions and similar obligations
- Taxation, including deferred taxation
- Other provisions

Accruals and deferred income

Capital and reserves

Called up share capital

Share premium account

Revaluation reserve

Other reserves
- Capital redemption reserve
- Reserve for own shares
- Reserves provided for and by the articles of association
- Other reserves

Profit and loss account

Minority interests

2

UK, Profit and Loss Account, Format 1

Turnover
Cost of sales
Gross profit or loss
Distribution costs
Administrative expenses
Other operating income
Income from interests in group undertakings
Income from interests in associated undertakings
Income from other participating interests
Income from other fixed asset investments
Other interest receivable and similar income
Amounts written off investments
Interest payable and similar charges
Profit or loss on ordinary activities before tax
Tax on profit or loss on ordinary activities
Profit or loss on ordinary activities after taxation
Profit or loss on ordinary activities attributable to minority interests
Extraordinary income
Extraordinary charges
Extraordinary profit or loss
Tax on extraordinary profit or loss
Profit or loss on extraordinary activities attributable to minority interests
Other taxes not shown under the above items
Profit or loss for the financial year

3

UK, Profit and Loss Account, Format 2

Turnover
Change in stocks of finished goods and in work in progress
Own work capitalised
Other operating income
Raw materials and consumables
Other external charges
Staff costs:
(*a*) wages and salaries
(*b*) social security costs
(*c*) other pension costs
Depreciation and other amounts written off tangible and intangible fixed assets
Exceptional amounts written off current assets
Other operating charges
Income from shares in group undertakings
Income from shares in associated undertakings
Income from other fixed asset investments
Amounts written off investments
Interest payable and similar charges
Profit or loss on ordinary activities before tax
Tax on profit or loss on ordinary activities
Profit or loss on ordinary activities after taxation
Profit or loss on ordinary activities attributable to minority interests
Extraordinary income
Extraordinary charges
Extraordinary profit or loss
Profit or loss on ordinary activities before tax
Tax on extraordinary profit or loss
Profit or loss on extraordinary activities attributable to minority interests
Other taxes not shown under the above items
Profit or loss for the financial year

4

Netherlands, Balance Sheet, Format A

Balance sheets as at

Fixed assets

Intangible fixed assets
share issue expenses
research and development
concessions and licenses
intellectual property rights
goodwill
payment on account

Tangible fixed assets
land and buildings
plant and machinery
fixtures, fittings, tools and equipment
in the course of construction and payments on account
not employed in the production process

Fixed asset investments
group companies
amounts owed by group companies
other participating interests
amounts owed by related companies
other investments
other loans

Total fixed assets

Current assets

Stocks
raw materials and consumables
work in progress
finished goods and goods for sale
payments on account

Debtors
trade debtors
amounts owed by group companies
amounts owed by related companies
other debtors
called up share capital not paid
prepayments and accrued income

Investments
shares, or depositary receipts thereof, in group companies
other investments

Cash at bank, giro and in hand

Total current assets

Current liabilities

Creditors due within one year
convertible debentures and other loans
other debentures and private loans
amounts owed to credit institutions
advance payments received on orders
trade creditors and trade credits
bills of exchange and cheques payable
amounts owed to group companies
amounts owed to related companies
taxation and social security
pensions
other creditors
accruals and deferred income

Net current assets

Total assets less current liabilities

Long-term liabilities

Creditors due after more than one year
convertible debentures and other loans
other debentures and private loans
amounts owed to credit institutions
advance payments received on orders
trade creditors and trade credits
bills of exchange and cheques payable
amounts owed to group companies
amounts owed to related companies
taxation and social security
pensions
other creditors
accruals and deferred income

Provisions for liabilities and charges

pensions
taxation
other

Capital and reserves

Paid up and called up share capital

Share premium account

Revaluation reserve

Statutory reserves and articles of association reserves
statutory reserves
articles of association reserves

Other reserves

Undistributed profit

5

Netherlands, Profit and Loss Account, Format E

Net turnover

Change in stocks of finished goods and work in progress
Own work capitalised
Other operating income

Total operating income

Raw materials
Work contracted out and other external expenses
Salaries and wages
Social security
Amortisation, depreciation and diminution in value of intangible and tangible fixed assets
Exceptional diminution in value of current assets
Other operating expenses

Total operating expenses

Operating profit or loss

Profit or loss on fixed asset investments
Other interest receivable and similar income
Profit or loss on participating interests
Increase in value of remaining fixed asset investments and current investments
Decrease in value of remaining fixed asset investments and current investments
Interest payable and similar expenses

Balance of financial income and expense

Profit or loss on ordinary activities before taxation

Tax on profit or loss on ordinary activities

Profit or loss on ordinary activities after taxation

Extraordinary income
Extraordinary expense

Extraordinary profit or loss before taxation

Tax on extraordinary profit or loss

Extraordinary profit or loss after taxation

Profit or loss after taxation

6

Netherlands, Profit and Loss Account, Format F

Net turnover

Cost of sales

Gross margin on turnover

Distribution expenses
General administrative expenses

Total expenses

Net margin on turnover

Other operating income

Operating profit and loss

Profit or loss on fixed asset investments
Other interest receivable and similar income
Profit or loss on participating interests
Increase in value of remaining fixed asset investments and current investments
Decrease in value of remaining fixed asset investments and current investments
Interest payable and similar expenses

Balance of financial income and expense

Profit or loss on ordinary activities before taxation

Tax on profit or loss on ordinary activities

Profit or loss on ordinary activities after taxation

Extraordinary income
Extraordinary expense

Extraordinary profit or loss before taxation

Profit or loss after taxation

7

France, Balance Sheet

Assets

Issued share capital not called

Fixed Assets

- Intangible fixed assets
  - Formation costs
  - Research and development costs
  - Concessions, patents, licences, trademarks, and similar rights and assets
  - Goodwill
  - Other intangible fixed assets
  - Payments on account

- Tangible fixed assets
  - Land
  - Buildings
  - Plant, machinery, tools
  - Other tangible fixed assets
  - Tangible fixed assets in course of construction
  - Payments on account

- Investments
  - Shares in group and related companies
  - Amounts owed by group and related companies
  - Other fixed asset investments
  - Other loans
  - Other investments

Current Assets

- Stocks and work in progress
- Raw materials and consumables
- Work in progress (goods & services)
- Intermediate and finished goods
- Goods for resale

Payments on account and deposits

Debtors
- Trade debtors
- Other debtors
- Called up share capital not paid

Investments
- Own shares
- Other investments

Cash at bank and in hand

Prepayments and Accrued Income
- Prepayments
- Accrued income

Debenture redemption premiums

Translation differences

Capital and liabilities

Capital and Reserves

- Share capital (of which paid up . . .)
- Share premiums
- Revaluation reserves
- Reserves:
  - Legal reserve
  - Reserves required by articles or by contract
  - Reserves required by regulations
  - Other (optional) reserves
- Carry forward from profit and loss account
  - (credit or debit balance)
  - Profit or loss for the accounting period

Sub-total: Net worth

Investment subsidies

Provisions required by regulations

Provisions for Liabilities and Charges
- Provisions for liabilities
- Provisions for charges

Creditors
- Convertible debenture loans
- Other debenture loans
- Loans and sundry creditors
- Payments received on account
- Trade creditors
- Debts relating to fixed assets
- Taxation and social security
- Other creditors
- Accruals and deferred income

Translation differences

8

France, Profit and Loss Account, Two-sided Version

Expenses	**Income**
Operating expenses	*Operating income*
Purchases of goods for resale	Sales of goods bought for resale
Variation in stocks thereof	Sales of goods and services produced
Purchases of raw materials and consumables	Net turnover (including exports)
Variation in stocks thereof	Variation in stock of finished goods and work in progress
Other purchases and external charges	Work performed for own purposes and capitalised
Taxes and similar payments	Operating subsidies
Wages and salaries	Provisions written back
Social security costs	Other operating income
Valuation adjustments	
on fixed assets: depreciation	
on fixed assets: other amounts written off	
on current assets: amounts written off	
relating to provisions for liabilities and charges	
Other operating expenses	
TOTAL operating expenses	TOTAL operating income
Share of loss on joint ventures	*Share of profit on joint ventures*
Financial expenses	*Financial income*
Value adjustments	From participating interests
Interest and similar expenses	From other investments and loans forming part of the fixed assets
Losses on foreign exchange	Other interest receivable and similar income
Net loss on transfers of short-term securities	Provisions written back
	Gains on foreign exchange
	Net gain from transfers of short-term securities
TOTAL financial expenses	TOTAL financial income
Exceptional expenses	*Exceptional income*
Operating	Operating
Non-operating	Non-operating
Depreciation and other amounts written off	Provisions written back
TOTAL exceptional expenses	TOTAL exceptional income
Profit share of employees	
Tax on profit	
TOTAL expenses	TOTAL income
Balance–profit	Balance–loss
SUM TOTAL	SUM TOTAL

9

Germany, Balance Sheet

Fixed assets

Intangible assets
- Concessions, industrial and similar rights and assets and licences in such rights and assets;
- Goodwill
- Payments on account

Tangible assets
- Land, land rights and buildings including buildings on third party land
- Technical equipment and machines
- Other equipment, factory and office equipment
- Payments on account and assets under construction

Financial assets
- Shares in affiliated enterprises
- Loans to affiliated enterprises
- Participations
- Loans to enterprises in which participations are held
- Long-term investments
- Other loans

Current Assets

Inventories
- Raw materials and supplies
- Work in process
- Finished goods and merchandise
- Payments on account

Receivables and other assets
- Trade receivables
- Receivables from affiliated enterprises
- Receivables from enterprises in which participations are held
- Other assets

Securities
- Shares in affiliated enterprises
- Own shares
- Other securities

Cheques, cash-in-hand, central bank and postal giro balances, bank balances

Prepaid

Equity

Subscribed capital
Capital reserves
Revenue reserves
- Legal reserve
- Reserve for own shares
- Statutory reserves
- Other revenue reserves

Retained profits/accumulated losses brought forward

Net income/net loss for the year

Accruals

Accruals for pensions and similar obligations
Tax accruals
Other accruals

Liabilities

Loans
- of which convertible:

Liabilities to banks
Payments received on account of orders
Trade payables
Liabilities on bills accepted and drawn
Payable to affiliated enterprises
Payable to enterprises in which participations are held
Other liabilities,
- of which taxes:
- of which relating to social security and similar obligations:

Deferred income

10

Germany, Profit and Loss Account, First Format

Sales
Increase or decrease in finished goods inventories and work in process
Own work capitalised
Other operating income
Cost of materials:
  Cost of raw materials, consumables and supplied and of purchased merchandise
  Cost of purchased services
Personnel expenses:
  Wages and salaries
  Social security and other pension costs,
    of which in respect of old age pensions:
Depreciation:
  On intangible fixed assets and tangible assets as well as on capitalised start-up and business expansion expenses
  On current assets to the extent that it exceeds depreciation which is normal for the company
Other operating expenses
Income from participations,
  of which from affiliated enterprises:
Income from other investments and long-term loans,
  of which relating to affiliated enterprises;
Other interest and similar income,
  of which from affiliated enterprises:
Amortisation of financial assets and investments classified as current assets
Interest and similar expenses,
  of which to affiliated enterprises:
Results from ordinary activities
Extraordinary income
Extraordinary expense
Extraordinary results
Taxes on income
Other taxes
Net income/net loss for the year

11

Germany, Profit and Loss Account, Second Format

Sales
Cost of sales
Gross profit on sales
Selling expenses
General administration expenses
Other administration expenses
Other operating income
Other operating expenses
Income from participations,
 of which from affiliated enterprises:
Income from other investments and financial assets,
 of which from affiliated enterprises:
Other interest and similar income,
 of which from affiliated enterprises:
Amortisation of financial assets and investments classified as current assets
Interest and similar expenses
 of which to affiliated enterprises:
Results from ordinary activities
Extraordinary income
Extraordinary expense
Extraordinary results
Taxes on income
Other taxes
Net income/net loss for the year

CHAPTER 6

The Valuation of Assets

This chapter looks at some major European differences in the methods for valuing assets in the balance sheets of companies. This is a vital matter because it directly affects the calculation of totals such as net assets, total assets, shareholders' funds, total capital, and so on. In order to assess the profitability of one company in comparison with another, at least one of these aggregate measures will be necessary. Given that assets are valued differently, international comparisons lack much meaning unless some adjustment is made for this.

The differences discussed in this chapter exist despite the harmonisation of accounting in the EC, caused by the Fourth Directive on company law. In order to get international agreement, the Directive had to contain compromises and options. This is particularly obvious in the area of asset valuation, where many alternatives exist for member states.

Topics which are more closely related to the measurement of profit are dealt with in Chapter 7. The inter-related matters of consolidation, currency translation and segmental reporting are left for Chapter 8. Readers are directed to Appendices I and II for a full reproduction of French and German notes on asset valuations.

6.1 Tangible Fixed Assets

It is easier to put a reliable value on tangible fixed assets (such as land, buildings or machines) than on intangibles (such as patents, licences or trade marks). Nevertheless, there are still many ways in which valuation can be done, and predominant practice differs country by country across Europe.

Section 2.5 used tangible fixed assets as an example of valuation differences, and the discussion there can serve as an introduction. It is pointed out there that historical cost is the traditional method of asset valuation in most countries. Some European countries are looked at in more detail below:

(*i*) *Germany*: Strict historical cost, except for write-downs for depreciation and other tax-allowed reductions, and for permanent diminutions in value. These points apply to most countries and will not be repeated.

(*ii*) *France*: Historical cost, except that assets were revalued in 1978 at 1976 values in a tax-exempt way, subsequent depreciation being based on these values (see box below). For group accounts, valuations can move away from these tax-controlled numbers.

1 VALUATION OF FIXED ASSETS (France, Total Oil, 1987)

'Fixed Assets—1976 Revaluation

Gross fixed assets of the French companies are included in the consolidated balance sheet at their book values. Fixed assets revalued by these companies in **1978** are accordingly included at their revised value.

In order to ensure consistency in the revaluation of Group assets, revaluations carried out by the foreign subsidiaries (but not incorporated in their own accounts), which are based upon the methods used by the French companies, have been included in the consolidated balance sheet.' [A less detailed note is included in the 1992 accounts in the Appendix I].

(*iii*) *Italy, Spain, Greece*: Somewhat similar to France, with tax-induced revaluations up to 1983 in Spain and as recently as 1990 and 1991 in Italy.

(*iv*) *Switzerland*: Historical cost, except that consolidated accounts are not compulsory so that no valuation rules apply. For example, Ciba-Geigy have been using current cost in their group accounts (see box below).

CURRENT VALUE (Switzerland, Ciba-Geigy)

'In the Summary of Financial Results, both sales on the one hand and expenses and costs on the other are stated at current value. Depreciation at current value assists in the maintenance of physical capital, and the appearance of paper profits in the accounts is avoided.

The current value principle is applied to the Summary of Financial Status by means of adjustments to the fixed assets and revaluation of stocks.'

(*v*) *Sweden*: Historical cost, except that revaluation is permitted when there has been a permanent increase in value (valuation does not normally exceed 75% of current value).

(*vi*) *UK, Ireland*: Historical cost, or current cost or market value (need not be current). Valuations can be, and for large companies often are, done on an *ad hoc* basis. However, there must be disclosure of the basis of valuation and what the historical cost would have been.

(*vii*) *Netherlands*: Somewhat like the UK, except that some companies use replacement cost as the main basis of valuation.

Chapters 1 and 2 examine the effect of taxation on asset valuation in most continental countries. This can lead to valuations which are far removed from commercial reality.

The Fourth Directive requires the disclosure of valuations that are determined by tax rules rather than by commercial or company law provisions. It is becoming increasingly easy to detect major instances of this, as the following German example shows:

DISCLOSURE OF TAX-BASED VALUATIONS (Germany, Daimler-Benz)

Special tax-deductible depreciation allowances amount to DM 77 million (1990: DM 95 million); depreciation in excess of scheduled depreciation amounts to DM 39 million (1990: DM 2 million).

A particular quirk of the UK and Ireland is that the relevant accounting standard (SSAP 19) requires investment properties to be annually revalued and not to be subject to systematic depreciation. In other countries investment properties are not treated differently from other properties.

6.2 Intangible Assets

Practice in this area varies greatly from country to country, and within a country. Goodwill on consolidation is a particular problem which is left for Chapter 8.

For example, in Germany it was normal until the end of 1987 (when the EC Fourth Directive came into force) to write many intangible assets off to zero on purchase (see box below). This is still possible outside the EC. At the other extreme, in the late 1980s, some UK companies began to value and capitalise internally developed brand names. The valuation method appears to be current cost, which is legal.

2 INTANGIBLES (Germany, AEG)

'Under the *intangible assets*, patents and similar rights acquired in 1987 are valued for the first time at cost, less scheduled amortization' (ie they were valued at zero before).

In general, however, intangible assets are valued, like other fixed assets, at historical cost less depreciation.

Under certain conditions, development expenditure can be capitalised and written off over its useful economic life in some countries (eg UK, France, Sweden, Spain and the Netherlands) but cannot be in others (eg Germany).

Formation expenses may be capitalised and written off over five years in France, Germany, the Netherlands and Spain, but must not be capitalised in the UK and Ireland.

6.3 Stocks (Inventories)

The 'lower of cost and market' rule is used throughout Europe, as a means of ensuring the prudent valuation of stock. It is required by the EC Fourth Directive. In most countries 'market' means net realisable value, but it can mean other valuations; for example, in Germany and Spain, replacement cost would be used where this is even lower than historical cost or net realisable value. In the Netherlands some companies value at the lower of replacement cost and net realisable value.

The determination of cost may involve the use of FIFO (first in, first out), LIFO (last in, first out), weighted average or some other method. In the UK, Ireland, France and Sweden, LIFO is not allowed for tax or accounting purposes (although it is allowed in group accounts in France). In Germany, LIFO is allowed where it corresponds to physical usage. In the Netherlands, LIFO is allowed but unusual. The treatment of overheads can vary. In most countries, only production overheads are included, but in Germany and Sweden the appropriate proportion of administration overheads may also be included.

Long-term contracts are accounted for on the percentage-of-completion method in the UK, Ireland and the Netherlands; this allows a proportion of profit to be taken as production proceeds. By contrast, the recording of profit usually waits for completion in France, Germany and Sweden.

Table 6.1 summarises some of these points.

6.4 Debtors

As a result of prudence, debtors are valued in all countries with reference to future expected receipts rather than to legal obligations outstanding. Specific and general provisions for doubtful debts are deducted from debtors and charged as expenses. For countries within the EC, the Fourth Directive requires separate disclosure of any amounts included under debtors (and therefore under 'current assets') that are not expected to be received within a year from the balance sheet date.

In some countries, such as Germany and Italy, there may be a tendency to increase general provisions because these are tax deductible. Also, in some countries, such as Italy, conventional individual company accounts show provisions for bad debts as a liability item rather than as a deduction from the asset debtors.

Foreign currency debtors in a company's balance sheet might be shown at either the transaction rate or the balance sheet rate. In the UK, Ireland and the Netherlands the balance sheet rate is used. The transaction rate would be regarded as irrelevant; and the balance sheet rate as the better guess for the future settlement rate.

In Germany and Sweden, foreign currency debtors are valued at the lower of the amounts that would be calculated under the transaction and balance sheet rates. This is a further example of conservatism. In France, company

Table 6.1 Predominant Inventory Valuation Techniques

UK, Ireland, France	Lower of FIFO and net realisable value.
Germany	Lowest of FIFO, net realisable value, current replacement cost or other value allowed by tax laws. Sometimes LIFO is used.
Italy	Lower of LIFO and net realisable value.
Sweden	Lowest of FIFO, net realisable value and current replacement cost. Generally, a 3% tax-deductible obsolescence provision is also taken off.
Spain	Lowest of FIFO, net realisable value and current replacement cost.
Switzerland	Lower of average cost and current replacement cost or (for finished goods) net realisable value. It is not necessary to include production overheads, but it is usual to take general provisions of up to one third.

accounts and tax accounts use transaction rates, but group accounts may use the closing rate.

Some of these points are illustrated in section 2.3.

6.5 Net Assets

Analysts will often be interested in arriving at a total of 'net assets', which is usually the same as 'shareholders' funds' (except that minority interests are not usually included in the latter but should probably be included in the former).

Clearly, all the points above in this chapter will affect these totals, but there are further problems relating to exactly which 'liabilities' to deduct in the calculation of net assets. This point was illustrated for France in section 2.4, where it was seen that some provisions are really reserves, meaning that they should not be included in shareholders' funds and not deducted in the calculation of net assets. (Provisions and reserves are discussed further in section 7.2.)

A German illustration was also begun by looking at the income statement effects (in Table 2.1). Table 6.2 opposite shows the capital and liabilities side of a German consolidated balance sheet (the full balance sheet is shown in Appendix II). The very large figure for 'Other provisions' prompts the question of how much of these provisions are like the 'provisions for contingencies' in section 2.4, ie how much are really 'reserves' in UK jargon. Sadly, it is exceptionally difficult to disentangle the total. What is clear from the notes is that large scale provision movements occur.

Table 6.2 Extract from Consolidated Balance Sheet of Daimler-Benz, 31 December 1992

Stockholders' Equity	
Capital Stock	2,330
Paid-In Capital	2,117
Retained Earnings	13,440
Minority Interests	1,228
Unappropriated Profit of Daimler-Benz AG	604
	19,719
Provisions	
Provisions for Old-Age Pensions and Similar Obligations	12,217
Other Provisions	22,478
	34,695

For example in 1992, Daimler-Benz note:

> **Other Operating Income**
>
> The income amount included in this caption for the reversal of provisions totals DM 1,519 million (1991: DM 893 million).

This is in the context of a net income for 1992 of DM 1,451 million. In 1993, the disclosure made by Daimler-Benz in the Form 20-F for SEC registration purposes show major provision movements. Extracts from Daimler-Benz 1992 accounts are included as Appendix II.

The 'Provisions for Old-Age Pensions' are not part of shareholders' funds. In a UK company, they would be separately held in a pension trust or in an independent company. A complication arises in that the pension fund may in some countries be over- or under-provided. If it is over-provided, part of it is really reserves. This is discussed and illustrated in section 7.4. Incidentally, if DM $22\frac{1}{2}$ bn of the provisions are for pensioners, this implies that DM $22\frac{1}{2}$ bn of the total assets (and the income on them) are for pensioners.

Starting from the top of the 'Stockholders' Equity' in Table 6.2, it is clear that the first three items are part of shareholders' funds. The implication of the order of items is that 'Minority Interests' are also part of shareholders' funds. However, this results from the German 'entity view' that sees the parent shareholders and the minority shareholders as joint contributors to the capital. For analysts from most countries, minorities are excluded.

The 'Unappropriated Profit of Daimler-Benz AG' of DM 604 million is waiting to be approved by the AGM for dividend distribution. UK practice would already have accrued for this by removing the amount from equity and adding it to current liabilities. Consequently, it is not part of shareholders' funds, according to a UK comparison.

Table 6.3 Calculation of Shareholders' Funds for Daimler-Benz

	DM m
Capital Stock	2,330
Paid-in Capital	2,117
Retained Earnings	13,440
Other Provisions	?
	———

Table 6.3 summarises the discussion. Incidentally, readers will have noticed the use of US terminology by Daimler-Benz. UK terminology for the first three items of Table 6.2 would be 'called up share capital', 'share premium account' and 'profit and loss account'.

An item which appears below shareholders' funds in some German companies is 'Special Untaxed Reserves' or 'Reserve Items with an Equity Element'. These are amounts that have been charged against income in order to obtain tax relief. They are not commercial expenses, so they are indeed 'reserves' in UK terminology. They should form part of shareholders' funds. There is one question, though: is it relevant that they would be taxable if they were to be returned back through the income statement in order to be distributed as dividends? If so, the tax rate on distributed income should be deducted (36% at the time of writing). As seen in Table 6.4 below, the Swedish accountancy body does think it relevant, but we could also ask: does the fact that a company cannot distribute share capital mean that the latter is not part of shareholders' funds? In other words: what is the relevance of distributability or distribution?

A further example of untaxed reserves may be useful. It is in Scandinavian countries that some of the greatest tax effects can be seen, so Sweden is taken as illustration here. Volvo, since it is registered with the SEC in the US, has to provide a reconciliation with US generally accepted accounting principles. Table 6.5 opposite shows such a reconciliation, including the note on untaxed reserves. This relates to several years ago. More recently, Sweden has changed this practice. Nevertheless, differences remain large. The Volvo figures for 1990 are shown as Table 6.6, and the analagous figures for the Norwegian company, Norsk Hydro, for 1992 are shown as Table 6.7.

Table 6.4 Extract from 'The Concise Key to Understanding Swedish Financial Statements' FAR, 1986

'Adjustments

Swedish financial statements can be basically adjusted to reflect US accounting principles as follows:

—Increase reported net income by 48% of the year's transfers to untaxed reserves; and

—Increase reported shareholders' equity by 48% of untaxed reserves in the balance sheet.

52% of each of these items represents deferred taxes.'

Table 6.5 Extract from Volvo's Reconciliation to US GAAP

Net Income	**1986**	**1985**
Net income as reported in the Consolidated Statements of Income (in accordance with Swedish accounting principles)	2,551	2,546
Items increasing (decreasing) reported income:		
Allocations to untaxed reserves (Note A)	2,694	3,330
Income taxes	(1,547)	(1,975)
Tooling costs	110	323
Equity method investments	113	122
Write-down of investments	(500)	—
Business combinations	80	192
Foreign currency translation	(530)	(808)
Other	(15)	4
Net increase in income before extraordinary income	405	1,188
Income before extraordinary income	2,956	3,734
Extraordinary income	—	744
Approximate net income in accordance with US GAAP	2,956	4,478
Per share amounts, SEK:		
Income before extraordinary income	38.10	48.10
Extraordinary income	—	9.60
Approximate net income per share in accordance with US GAAP	38.10	57.70
Weighted average number of shares outstanding (in thousands)	77,605	77,605
Shareholders' equity		
Shareholders' equity as reported in the Consolidated Balance Sheets (in accordance with Swedish accounting principles)	10,124	8,798
Items increasing (decreasing) reported shareholders' equity:		
Untaxed reserves (Note A)	20,980	17,738
Income taxes	(11,950)	(10,279)
Tooling costs	1,269	1,159
Equity method investments	(233)	211
Business combinations	(282)	35
Other	184	142
Net increase in reported shareholders' equity	9,968	9,006
Approximate shareholders' equity in accordance with US GAAP	20,092	17,804

Note A. Allocations to untaxed reserves

Tax legislation in Sweden and certain other countries permits companies to make allocations to untaxed reserves, which are used principally to strengthen a company's financial position through the deferral of income taxes. To qualify as a tax deduction, Swedish tax law requires that these allocations must be deducted for financial reporting purposes. In accordance with US GAAP, such allocations are not recognized as a reduction of income for financial reporting purposes.

Table 6.6 Volvo's US GAAP Reconciliation, 1990

Application of US GAAP would have the following approximate effect on consolidated net income and shareholders' equity of the group:

Net income (loss)	
Net income (loss) in accordance with Swedish accounting principles	(1,020)
Items increasing (decreasing) reported income:	
Income taxes (Note A)	58
Tooling costs (Note B)	718
Interest costs (Note C)	140
Business combinations (Note D)	(50)
Foreign currency translation (Note E)	(51)
Leasing (Note F)	41
Other (Note G)	141
Net increase in net income	997
Approximate net income (loss) in accordance with US GAAP	(23)
Approximate net income (loss) per share in accordance with US GAAP, SEK	(0.30)
Weighted average number of shares outstanding (in thousands)	77,605
Shareholders' equity	
Shareholders' equity in accordance with Swedish accounting principles	35,291
Items increasing (decreasing) reported shareholders' equity:	
Income taxes (Note A)	(7,133)
Tooling costs (Note B)	2,706
Interest costs (Note C)	391
Business combinations (Note D)	196
Leasing (Note F)	(278)
Other (Note G)	257
Net decrease in shareholders' equity	(3,861)
Approximate shareholders' equity in accordance with US GAAP	31,430

Table 6.7 Norsk Hydro's US GAAP Reconciliation, 1992

Reconciliation of net income stated in accordance with US GAAP to net income stated in accordance with Norwegian accounting principles

Amounts in NOK million	**US GAAP**	**N GAAP**
Operating income US GAAP	2,881	2,881
Adjustments for N GAAP:		
Raw materials—Capitalized costs (b) (c)		(314)
Depreciation (b) (c) (d)		618
Other operating costs		396
Operating income N GAAP		3,581
Equity in net income of non-consolidated investees	126	126
Restated for N GAAP deferred tax (a)		
Financial income (expense) US GAAP	(2,616)	(2,616)
Adjustments for N GAAP		
Capitalised interest (d)		(658)
Foreign exchange gains (e)		463
Other income (expense), net	176	176
Extraordinary income (expense)		413
Income (loss) before taxes and minority interest—N GAAP		1,485
Current income tax expense	(439)	(439)
Deferred income tax expense	(239)	(239)
Adjusted to N GAAP deferred tax (g)		(556)
Minority interest	(84)	(84)
Cumulative effect of accounting changes	1,958	
Net income (loss)	1,763	167

Reconciliation of shareholders' equity stated in accordance with US GAAP to shareholders' equity stated in accordance with Norwegian accounting principles

Amounts in NOK million	**US GAAP**	**N GAAP**
Shareholders' equity for US GAAP		20,164
Prepaid expenses and other current assets		66
Investments (a)		—
Property, plant and equipment—Capitalised costs (b) (c) (d)		(8,097)
Non-current assets		(18)
Dividends payable (h)		(616)
Unrealised exchange gains—current and long-term (e)		(1,340)
Other long-term liabilities		—
Deferred tax assets and liabilities—current and long-term (g)		6,248
Shareholders' equity for N GAAP		16,407

Table 6.7 (continued)

Explanation of major differences between N GAAP and US GAAP

(a) Accounting change: As discussed in Note 1, prior years' N GAAP consolidated financial statements have been restated for accounting changes for pensions and deferred taxes which have the following impact on Shareholders' equity:

Amounts in NOK million	**1 January 1990**
1 January, 1990, as previously reported	7,693
Restatement for accounting change for:	
Prior years' effect of pensions	1,911
Prior years' effect of deferred taxes	6,683
1 January, 1990, as restated	16,287

Net income was restated as follows:

Amounts in NOK million	**Year ended 31 December 1991**	**1990**
Net income as previously reported	(2,169)	2,044
Restatement for accounting change for:		
Pensions	367	457
Deferred taxes	1,127	185
Net income, as restated	(675)	2,686

(b) Exploration drilling costs: Under N GAAP, all exploration costs are expensed as incurred. Under US GAAP, exploration drilling costs are capitalised provided drilling results in proved reserves. They are amortised as depletion expense when production begins.

(c) Environmental costs: Under N GAAP, environmental related expenditures were expensed as incurred through 1991. Under US GAAP, environmental related expenditures which increase the life or improve the safety of a facility are capitalised and amortised through depreciation expense. Beginning in 1992, environmental costs for N GAAP are recorded consistently with US GAAP and the difference represents the amortisation of previous years' capitalised costs for US GAAP.

(d) Capitalised interest: All interest is expensed as incurred for N GAAP. Under US GAAP, interest is capitalised for major constructed assets and amortised as part of depreciation expense.

(e) Unrealised exchange gains: Under N GAAP, unrealised exchange gains on foreign currency assets, liabilities and financial instruments are deferred as current or long-term liabilities. Unrealised gains on non-current assets and long-term liabilities are deferred only to the extent they exceed unrealised losses in the same currency.

All unrealised exchange gains are recognised as financial income for US GAAP.

Unrealised exchange losses are expensed for both N GAAP and US GAAP.

(f) Commodities contracts: Under N GAAP, unrealised gains and losses for purchase and forward commodities contracts are netted as a portfolio and net unrealised exchange gains are deferred as other long-term liabilities. Unrealised gains are recognised under other operating expenses for US GAAP.

(g) Deferred taxes: Under N GAAP, deferred taxes are recorded based upon the liability method similar to US GAAP. Differences occur primarily because items accounted for differently under US GAAP (capitalised exploration drilling costs, capitalised interest, unrealised exchange gains, etc.) also have deferred tax effects.

N GAAP also has more stringent criteria for recognising deferred tax assets.

Under N GAAP, offsetting deferred tax assets and liabilities for each tax entity are netted and classified as a long-term liability. Under N GAAP, tax assets primarily related to unfunded pension plans and post retirement benefits are classified as long-term assets. Disclosure of the current and long-term temporary differences giving rise to the N GAAP deferred tax asset and liability is provided in Note 9.

Classification between current and long-term for US GAAP is determined by the classification of the related asset or liability giving rise to the temporary difference. For each tax entity, deferred tax assets and liabilities are offset within the respective current or long-term groups and presented as a single amount. A reconciliation of deferred tax assets and liabilities from US GAAP to N GAAP as of 31 December 1992 follows.

	31 December 1992	
Amounts in NOK million	**Assets**	**Liabilities**
Gross deferred tax assets and liabilities, US GAAP	4,330	(18,096)
Adjustments for N GAAP:		
Exploration drilling costs		2,552
Capitalised interest		3,071
Unrealised exchange gains		479
Other		146
Gross deferred tax assets and liabilities, N GAAP	4,330	(11,848)
NET—N GAAP	173	(7,691)

(h) Dividends payable: For N GAAP, dividends proposed at the end of the year which will be declared and paid in the following year are recorded as a reduction to equity and as debt. For US GAAP, equity is reduced when dividends are declared and paid.

CHAPTER 7

Profit Measurement

Throughout Europe, the principles of prudence and accruals (matching) are used in profit measurement. These are specifically required by the EC's Fourth Directive, as is consistency of use of practices from year to year. Nevertheless, it is possible to give different emphases to these principles, and this is one reason why international differences in practice can result. In Chapter 6 the treatments of development expenditure and long-term contracts illustrate the conflict between accruals and prudence, and how it is resolved differently from country to country. This, and most other matters of valuation referred to earlier, affect profit measurement. A conservative valuation generally implies a conservative profit figure.

Several important areas of profit measurement are discussed below. As with valuation, most of the differences discussed in this chapter have survived EC harmonisation. Also, Appendices I and II contain reproduction of French and German company notes of relevance to this.

7.1 Depreciation

The basic divide in Europe is between those countries where depreciation in the financial statements is determined using accounting standards (eg the UK, Ireland and the Netherlands), and other countries where tax rules play an important part. To take the example of the UK, there is a quite separate system of capital allowances, which are depreciation allowances for tax purposes. They are set by Parliament in order to achieve various economic aims, such as the encouragement of investment in depressed regions. This separation allows tax depreciation to achieve these aims and to be objective in size, whereas accounting depreciation can be determined by the use of judgment about scrap values, useful lives and nature of wearing out.

In the Netherlands, depreciation for tax purposes usually follows accounting depreciation, although it can be different. In cases of difference in these countries, it can be said that 'reversible timing differences' arise. That is, usually the main difference between tax depreciation and accounting depreciation is the *timing* of it not the eventual total of it. Tax depreciation often runs faster than accounting depreciation. Reversible timing differences lead to deferred tax, as discussed in the next section.

In most European countries, the tradition is that one of the main purposes of accounting has been for the collection of tax. Tax rules have dominated accounting rules. In Germany, the identity of tax and accounting rules is described as the *Massgeblichkeitsprinzip*. For example, in those cases where there are rapid tax depreciation allowances for regional development purposes, these uncommercially large charges must be recorded in the accounts in order to be allowable for tax purposes.

In many cases the tax rules allow depreciation charges that are broadly in line with what accountants would choose based on economic and physical factors. However, there will frequently be small differences and sometimes very large differences.

To some extent there has been a move away from this tax domination since the late 1980s in some countries. For example, in France it is possible to correct for these tax influences in group accounts. Throughout the EC, the Fourth and Seventh Directives require at least the disclosure of the effects of taxation rules. Where tax and accounting depreciation are the same, there can be no cause of deferred taxation.

In some countries, it is possible to revalue assets, as discussed in section 6.1. In such cases, depreciation charges would normally be raised in line with the revaluation of the assets. However, in France, where a general revaluation took place in 1978, depreciation charges are still reduced back to historical cost in order not to reduce taxable income. In French group accounts, this equalisation can be eliminated.

One peculiar feature of UK practice, as discussed in Chapter 5, is the annual revaluation of investment properties. This also has an effect on depreciation because the rules (SSAP 19) require that there shall not be systematic depreciation charges for investment properties. Further, a fairly common UK treatment of hotels, stores and similar properties is that they are not depreciated where it can be shown that repair and maintenance expenses are sufficient to keep the properties in at least as good a condition as when they were bought.

7.2 Deferred Tax

In the previous section, reversible timing differences between tax and accounting depreciation were shown to be a cause of deferred taxation. Other causes of reversible timing differences might be inventory valuation methods or instalment sales. In some countries, such as the USA, these differences are fully accounted for. That is, to continue with the example of accelerated tax depreciation, tax liabilities could be said to be artificially low in early years. Accounting for deferred tax corrects for this, as a result of the accruals convention.

The technique for achieving full accounting for deferred tax is to increase (*debit*) the tax for the year in the income statement to what it would have been without the generous tax rules. The counter-balancing effect is to create a deferred tax account (*credit*), which one could interpret as a liability to pay more tax in the future. Both accounting entries may seem unattractive to management: the debit makes earnings look lower; the credit makes liabilities look worse.

In the UK and Ireland, many reversible timing differences arise but standard practice is *not* to account fully for deferred tax. The method used is partial allocation, whereby deferred tax is only recognised as a liability when it is expected to be paid within the foreseeable future (normally three years). Some Dutch and Italian companies also follow this practice.

In most of continental Europe, deferred tax is not a major problem because of the close relationship between tax and accounting figures. However, in consolidated accounts, there may be foreign elements of deferred tax. Furthermore, in France, for example, consolidated accounts can now be freed from the dominance of tax; and, when values are changed from those in the individual company accounts, deferred tax may arise.

Throughout Europe, it is normal to use the 'liability' method, that is to take account of changes in the corporation tax rate because this will affect the amounts of future tax paid.

7.3 Provisions and Reserves

This matter has already been discussed in Chapter 2, but more detail is given here. An initial problem to address is that the words 'provision' and 'reserve' are used rather loosely. In English, this is the case in North America, where a provision for bad debts may be called an allowance or a reserve. For continental European accounts, after translation into American or British English, the subtleties of these words are frequently lost.

In the UK, a provision is an expense. It is, in a sense, an anticipation of a future expense or loss which is at present uncertain in size or probability. However, it usually relates to a past event: a bad debt provision relates to a past sale; a depreciation provision to past wearing out; a provision for a law suit to past unfair dismissals, etc. The provision leads to a charge to profit and to the setting up of a provision account, which is a liability account or a reduction in an asset account.

By contrast, a reserve is merely an allocation of the profit that has already been calculated. The reserve will often indicate that profits must not be depreciated (eg the legal reserve discussed in section 2.3) or that the directors intend not to distribute the profits.

Consequently, the distinction between provisions and reserves is of great importance. The setting up of a £1m provision has the effects of lowering earnings by £1m and raising liabilities (lowering net assets) by £1m. The setting up of a £1m reserve has no effect on any aggregates or ratios that analysts think important.

The difficulty for international analysis is that some continental companies make so-called provisions for no specific contingency: provisions for contingencies, provisions for general risks. French and German examples of these were given in section 2.4. There are also tax-based reserves, which are treated as provisions. In order to gain advantage of some tax law, a company must charge income with non-commercial tax 'expenses'. Some examples of this are shown in the box opposite.

TAX-BASED PROVISION
(Germany, VEBA)

'(27) Other operating expenses

These expenses include additions to reserves subject to future taxation of DM 14.4 million, compared to DM 4.4 million in the previous year.'

(Germany, Henkel)

'The provision in the consolidated financial statements also includes corresponding amounts from the statements of other German companies, deferred tax liabilities of foreign companies, profits taxes on consolidation adjustments which will be subject to tax at later date, and the tax portion of special accounts and tax-allowable valuation adjustments still permitted under company law.'

Recently it has been possible in some countries to retain the advantage of tax-based provisions in company accounts, yet to move away from the accounting effects of this in consolidated accounts. In France, for example, although not all groups take advantage of this greater separation of tax from financial statements, it is normal for large listed companies. It is not normal for Germany.

7.4 Extraordinary Items

The definition of 'extraordinary' appears to be fixed in the Fourth Directive as 'otherwise than in the course of the company's ordinary activities'. However, in practice, the use of the term varies in Europe for several reasons:

(*i*) The Directive is not in force in some countries: such as (at the time of writing) Austria, Switzerland, Sweden, etc.
(*ii*) Some countries add glosses to the definition: eg in the UK and Ireland (FRS 3), extraordinary items must also be material and not expected to recur, and certain items (eg investment sales) are specifically stated not to be extraordinary.
(*iii*) Exactly what is 'ordinary activities' varies. For example, in the UK the sale of a shop by a stores group would not be thought to be extraordinary whereas it probably would be by a French stores group.

The example overleaf uses a public company in Denmark, where the Fourth Directive was implemented in 1981. Of the extraordinary expenses shown, only the second appears to fit the UK definition. Of the gains, the sale of tangible assets may well have been not extraordinary by UK standards.

EXTRAORDINARY ITEMS (Denmark, FLS Smidth & Co)

	KM
Note 5 Extraordinary income	
Profit on sale of site	144
Profits on sale of shares	50
Profits on sale of tangible assets	24
Other income	16
	234
Note 6 Extraordinary expenses	
Extraordinary losses on completed orders	44
Redundancy payments	35
Extraordinary write-offs on stocks and work in progress, etc.	31
Losses on sale of tangible assets	14
Losses on sale of properties	4
Other expenses	24
	152

(Note: the profit before extraordinaries was K 71M)

The important point is that analysts like to *exclude* extraordinary items. Analysts may well wish to standardise on this but will be frustrated because of the differing definition. It may be necessary to standardise on profit after extraordinary items, because this is immune from the effects of the definition of extraordinary.

A further complication is the use in the UK and Ireland of the term 'exceptional items' (see Table 7.1 opposite). These are amounts which are *not* thought to be outside ordinary activities but are abnormal in size or incidence. In French, both extraordinary and exceptional are translated as 'exceptionnel', which hardly helps international analysis.

7.5 Pensions

The provision for pension costs can be a very large expense for many companies. It has become standard practice in the UK and the US to base a year's pension on an actuarial assessment of the degree to which the work done in that particular year will give rise to eventual pension payments. That is, the pay-as-you-go basis is not acceptable; under that system, a new company with a pension scheme but no pensioners would appear to have no pension costs.

However, even between the UK and the US, the differences of technical detail can lead to large differences in yearly charges. This is all the more so

Table 7.1 Consolidated Profit and Loss Account of Marks and Spencer for the year ended 31 March 1992 (£m)

Turnover	5,793.4
Cost of sales	3,833.9
Gross Profit	1,959.5
Other expenses	1,283.7
Operating profit	675.8
Net interest receivable	10.8
Profit before profit sharing and taxation	686.6
Profit sharing	16.2
Profit before exceptional charges and taxation	670.4
Exceptional charges—UK	16.9
—Canada	30.0
Profit on ordinary activities before taxation	623.5
Tax on profit on ordinary activities	218.3
Profit on ordinary activities after taxation	405.2
Minority interests	2.6
Profit attributable to shareholders before extraordinary charges	402.6
Extraordinary charges—provision for loss on disposal of peoples	13.8
—goodwill	16.0
Profit for the financial year	372.8
Dividends	
Preference shares	0.1
Ordinary shares:	
Interim of 2.1p per share	57.4
Final of 5.0p per share	137.0
	194.5
Undistributed surplus	178.3
Earnings per share:	
Pre exceptional charges	16.3p
Post exceptional charges	14.8p

for differences between the UK and continental Europe. If the rules for pension costs are lax, it becomes possible to charge too much or too little for pensions, and thereby to manipulate profits. A summary for some countries is shown as Table 7.2.

Social conventions also affect this. The example in Table 7.3 overleaf uses

Table 7.2 Pension Provisions

Belgium	Not all commitments are fully funded. Unfunded amounts should be noted as contingencies; funded amounts externally funded.
Denmark	Commitments must be fully externally funded, except for directors' pensions.
France	The usual 'defined contribution' type are funded by industry schemes; expenses recorded as payments made. 'Defined benefit' plans do not need to be funded. Retirement bonuses are not generally funded.
Germany	Obligations arising before 1987 need not be provided for. Other obligations are generally internally provided for using tax-based assumptions (eg only for staff aged 30 or more, and a discount rate of 6%).
Italy	Pensions are paid by state, so generally no provisions are made. Severance pay is accrued.
Netherlands	Legally enforceable pension obligations must be covered by a life assurance company, industry pension fund or company trust fund.
Spain	Currently generated commitments must be fully funded, but accruals were not generally made until 1990. At present the unfunded amounts are being covered by 1/15th of past service cost each year for active employees and 1/7th per year for retired employees.
Switzerland	Full provision is not required, disclosure as contingent liabilities is sufficient. Any funding must be external.
UK	Commitments are generally fully externally funded.

UK, French and Italian companies. In all cases an amount has been charged, but the actual movement of funds may vary, which will certainly affect cash flow calculations based on income statements.

The British company places all pension provisions with a financial institution, and in this case, the 'funds' in question leave the company. For a company operating in France, there is a statutory requirement that part of the company's profits be allocated for the benefit of employees, with reinvestment in external assets within two years. In the short term, there is an element in Funds Generated from Operations (+F. 800 in the example) which is the accrual for the year, although only the cash outflow has actually been placed in external investments (−F. 700).

In Italy, employees are entitled on leaving a company to one month's salary (at current rates of pay) for each year in service. There is no requirement for the company to place these funds in earmarked investments, although the appropriate provisions must be made. Thus, Funds Generated from Operations includes the provision (+L. 80,000) net of the cash payment to retiring employees (−L. 30,000).

Table 7.3 Different Remuneration Methods and Funds Generated from Operations

	UK (£)	France (Francs)	Italy (Lire)
Earnings	100	1,000	100,000
Add back:			
Provision for employee pensions	80	—	—
less: funds applied in the current year	(80)	—	—
Share of profits attributable to employees	—	800	—
less: funds applied in the current year	—	(700)	—
Deferred employee remuneration	—	—	80,000
less: funds applied in the current year	—	—	(30,000)
Funds generated from operations*	100	1,100	150,000

*assuming no depreciation or other adjustments

Source: adapted from S J McLeay in C W Nobes and R H Parker, *Comparative International Accounting*, Prentice Hall, 1991.

7.6 The 'Bottom Line'

This chapter has shown that it will usually be misleading to concentrate on any single line near the end of a profit and loss account. Apart from the problems of profit measurement and definition, there are also differences in presentation. The positioning of extraordinary items, taxes, dividends, minority interests and reserves varies.

(*i*) *Extraordinaries*

In the UK and Ireland, extraordinaries are shown after 'profit on ordinary activities after taxation'. That is, tax is split between the amounts charged on ordinary and that on extraordinary profit. Table 7.1 shows an extract from a typical UK profit and loss account; the tax on extraordinary items could be shown on the face of the account but would normally be shown in a note. However, from the second half of 1993, extraordinary items are rare in the UK.

Table 7.4 Profit and Loss Account of FLS Group, 1987 (Denmark)

	KM
Net sales (Note 1)	**7,166**
Cost of sales (Note 1)	(5,590)
Gross profit	1,576
Income from shares in subsidiaries (Note 2)	—
Interest receivable (Note 3)	823
Interest payable (Note 3)	
Sales and distribution costs (Note 1)	(622)
Administrative costs (Note 1)	(1,119)
Other operating income	58
Income from shares in associated companies (Note 4)	127
Income from other investments	21
Result before extraordinary items and tax	**71**
Extraordinary income (Note 5)	234
Extraordinary expenses (Note 6)	(152)
Provision for special contingencies	—
Result before tax	**153**
Tax on income for the year (Note 7)	(80)
Result after tax	**73**
Minority interests' share	(2)
Net result for the year	**71**

In most other countries, extraordinaries are shown gross of taxation and above the tax charge (see Table 7.4 for Denmark, and Tables 7.5 or 2.1 for Germany).

In Germany, for example, there are several different types of taxes. So 'pre-tax' is ambiguous. (It should be noted that pre-tax profits in the UK are *after* some taxes, such as VAT and property rates.)

(*ii*) *Dividends*

In Tables 7.4 and 2.1, no dividends are shown as being paid. This is generally the case in continental Europe. In the UK and Ireland, a provision is made at the end of the year for the dividends proposed by the directors to be paid from the year's profits (see Table 7.1). This has to be approved by the AGM, but normally this is a formality. Therefore, the accruals convention suggests an accrual. In the accounts of a French company there are sometimes two columns in a balance sheet, showing 'before allocation' (or 'before AGM decisions') and after (see Appendix I).

Table 7.5 Consolidated Statement of Income of the Henkel Group

	1987	
	DM'000	**%**
Sales	9,255,915	100.0
Cost of sales	5,409,579	58.4
Gross profit	3,846,336	41.6
Selling and distribution costs	2,378,617	25.7
Research and development costs	277,307	3.0
Administrative expenses	592,844	6.4
Other operating income	82,968	0.9
Other operating charges	106,455	1.2
Operating result	574,081	6.2
Financial items	− 42,934	−0.5
Result from ordinary activities	531,147	5.7
Extraordinary items	− 35,874	−0.4
Taxes on income	−200,565	−2.2
Other taxes	− 2,708	—
Profit for the year	292,000	3.1
Allocation to revenue reserves	−195,887	−2.1
Minority interests in profits	− 21,424	−0.2
Minority interests in losses	+ 1,611	—
Consolidated unappropriated profit	76,300	0.8

(*iv*) *Minority Interests*

In some countries, for example Germany, the minority interests share of profit is not seen as a charge against earnings. This is because of the entity concept of the group or *Konzern*, that places less stress on the parent company shareholders. In Table 7.5, profit is shown before minorities. For most other countries, this is not the case: eg Denmark (Table 7.4) and the UK (Table 7.1). In the UK, minority share of profits is always extracted in the calculation of 'earnings'.

(v) *Reserves*

In Table 7.5, the German company's reserve movements take place with items that would be included in earnings in the UK. In Table 2.1, another German company includes them in 'Group result'. By contrast, in the UK, reserve movements are clearly separated, or may be relegated to the notes. In France, the two-column approach (see (iii) above) handles the problem.

Of course, with two-sided accounts it is much more difficult to see what is going on. Two-sided accounts are still presented for individual companies in most European countries. The French example in the appendix to Chapter 5 illustrates this.

CHAPTER 8

Group Accounting

As discussed in section 2.6, consolidation is an invention that is only slowly spreading through Europe. By the end of the 1980s, it was still a rarity in many countries, even some in the EC. So, it is particularly important to ascertain whether a set of accounts is consolidated or not. In the absence of consolidated accounts, useful analysis without further information is impossible (see discussion surrounding Tables 2.3 and 2.4).

Given that a set of consolidated financial statements is available, it is then possible to grapple with the many areas where there are important international differences in treatment.

8.1 The Scope of 'The Group'

The purpose of consolidation is to present the accounts of the group as if it were a single entity. However, the exact scope of the group, and whether to consolidate all of it are debatable matters. The first question is whether the group is a set of enterprises under common control or those under common ownership? The logic of group accounting makes it clear that control is what really matters. Consequently, there is no debate that 100% of the assets, income, etc of a subsidiary should be consolidated even if it is only 75% owned. That amount of ownership will allow 100% control. This also makes it clear, for example, that a foreign subsidiary should be excluded from consolidation if the foreign government restricts management or bans distribution of profits. Doubts about control and about international accounting differences led German law to allow the exclusion of all foreign subsidiaries (until 1990 year-ends). However, most countries include normal foreign subsidiaries.

Where there is a sub-subsidiary in which the group owns 36%, this could easily still be controlled (see S_{11} in Table 8.1 opposite). Furthermore, in Table 8.1 the 45% holding in S_2 could make it a subsidiary if the remaining shares were widely spread and in practice exercised no control. French law imposes a rebuttable presumption that holdings of even 40% imply parentage. Traditional practice in the Netherlands and France has been to stress control as the criterion for consolidation.

In the UK and Germany, by contrast, although control is seen as the reason for consolidation, ownership was seen as the most readily auditable proxy for the existence of control. Under the EC's Seventh Directive on company law (discussed in detail in Chapter 4) there are six identifiable

Table 8.1 A Group Structure

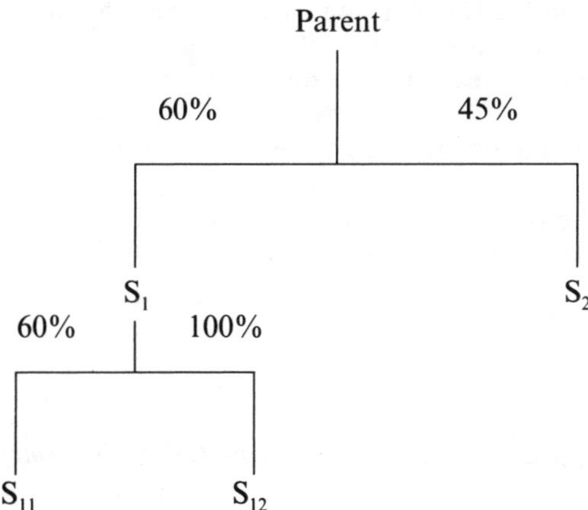

criteria for consolidation; most of them rest upon ownership. Table 8.2 overleaf shows the UK definitions. There are international differences even within the EC and after the Seventh Directive. Despite these differences, in most cases a subsidiary is a company in which the group holds more than half the voting shares.

8.2 Associates and Joint Ventures

Some enterprises are not fully controlled by a group but are, nevertheless, significantly influenced by it. It has gradually become standard international practice to account for investments in such companies by a form of partial consolidation, usually called the equity method or one-line consolidation. Under this method, instead of bringing into the group balance sheet only the

Table 8.2 Definitions of a Subsidiary (UK 1989 Act based on Seventh Directive)

Any one of the following will establish a parent/subsidiary relationship: where the parent,

1 (a) has the majority of voting rights; or
  (b) has the right to exercise dominant influence over the subsidiary because of a contract or provisions in the memorandum or articles; or

2 is a member of the subsidiary and
  (a) controls the majority of votes on the board of directors, or
  (b) controls by agreement the majority of voting rights; or

3 has a participating (20+%) interest and
  (a) exercises dominant influence, or
  (b) manages on a unified basis.

cost of the investment, the group's proportion of the equity (or net assets) of the enterprise is accounted for in a single line. In the UK and Ireland, such enterprises are called associates; in the US (and therefore by some continental countries) they are also called, for example, 'companies consolidated by the equity method'.

In the group profit and loss account, the equity method involves taking the group's proportion of the net profit and tax of the associate. The normal position for this is 'above the line'; that is, included in earnings. This can be seen for the UK in Table 8.3 and for Denmark in Table 7.4. However, there

Table 8.3 Consolidated Profit and Loss Account of J. Sainsbury plc, 1993

	1993 **£m**
Group Sales (including VAT & Sales Taxes)	10,269.7
VAT & Sales Taxes	584.2
Group Sales (excluding VAT & Sales Taxes)	9,685.5
Cost of Sales	8,688.9
Gross Profit	996.6
Administrative Expenses	211.6
Group Operating Profit	785.0
Associates—share of (loss)/profit	(0.4)
Profit Sharing	(58.6)
Loss on sale of properties	(2.4)
Profit on Ordinary Activities before Interest	723.6
Net Interest receivable	9.2
Profit on Ordinary Activities before Tax	732.8
Tax on Profit on Ordinary Activities	228.8
Profit on Ordinary Activities after Tax	504.0
Minority Interest	1.2
Profit for Financial Year	502.8
Dividends	177.3
Profit Retained	325.5

can be variation. For example, some, but not all, French companies show income from associates near the end of the profit and loss account, as in Table 8.4 below.

The exact definition of an associate can vary, but 'significant influence' is now generally presumed for investments of 20% to 50%. At one point in the Netherlands the threshold was 25% and in France 33⅓%, but the Seventh Directive is harmonising on 20%. In some countries, the equity method was illegal (as in Germany until 1987 year-ends) or just not used. However, the Seventh Directive makes it compulsory (for example, in Germany from 1990 year-ends). In Sweden, most companies do not use the equity method because of doubts about its legality, despite a statement from the accountancy body (FAR) suggesting that it is acceptable in consolidated accounts. In the case of Volvo, the appropriate adjustment to US GAAP is shown in Table 6.5.

Other non-EC countries are likely to follow the lead of the Seventh Directive. However, they have not always done so, as may be seen from the example overleaf, where associates are not treated by the equity method.

Table 8.4 Consolidated Statement of Income of Bull, 1987

	FF'000s
Revenue:	
Sales	10,412,006
Rental, service and other	7,659,199
Total	**18,071,205**
Costs and Expenses:	
Cost of revenue	(10,545,231)
Research and development	(1,551,539)
Selling, general and administrative	(5,487,076)
Interest expense	(845,118)
Interest income	242,622
Other income—net	314,645
Total	**(17,871,697)**
Profit before Income Taxes, Extraordinary Credit and Minority Interests	**199,508**
Provision for income taxes	(1,021,317)
Extraordinary credit – income tax benefits of loss carryforwards	985,645
Minority interests	(8,629)
Share of the results of companies consolidated by the equity method	69,634
Net Income	**225,201**

ASSOCIATES (Switzerland, Adia)

'**Scope.** The consolidated statements include the figures of affiliated companies (which close their books at year end), according to the following criteria:

(*a*) For companies in the service sector:
When Adia SA owns over 50%, assets, liabilities, revenues and expenses are taken into account for 100%. The profit attributable to minority interests is deducted from the consolidated net profit under the heading "Minority Interests".

When Adia SA owns 50% or less, the consolidation takes into account the value of the investment and the dividends paid as booked in Adia SA.

(*b*) For all other Group companies:
Irrespective of the percentage held, only the value of the investment and the dividends paid are treated in the consolidation.'

In many countries, joint ventures are treated as associates. However, the long-standing practice of some groups in France and the Netherlands is to use 'proportional consolidation' whereby the group's proportion of assets, liabilities, revenues and expenses are taken line-by-line into the group accounts. A typical note on this for a French company is reproduced below.

PROPORTIONAL CONSOLIDATION (France, Total Oil)

'Consolidation is, however, proportional, on the one hand for "joint interest" companies in which the holding is less than 50% and in which operations are shared on the basis of each partner's interest, and on the other hand for companies controlled jointly on a 50/50 basis by the Group and a single other shareholder.'

The Seventh Directive gives member states the option to allow proportional consolidation. This option has been taken, for example, in Germany, France and the Netherlands. However, in the UK the method is only available for unincorporated joint ventures.

8.3 Goodwill

Goodwill is the excess of the cost of an investment in a subsidiary (or associate or joint venture) over the proportion of net assets acquired. It has gradually become international practice for the net assets of the subsidiary to be measured at 'fair values' at the acquisition date for this purpose (as an estimate of 'cost' to the group). However, in most continental European countries, the traditional method was to compare the cost of investment with the *book* value of the group's share of the subsidiary's net assets. This means a larger goodwill figure. The Seventh Directive requires the use of fair values or a method that gives similar results that is now used in Germany (see Table 5.5). Nevertheless, the old method still continues in some European countries.

Once goodwill has been calculated, at least three subsequent treatments can be found:

(*i*) Leave the goodwill in the balance sheet at the acquisition level. This is not permissible under the Seventh Directive but is not unknown in Europe.
(*ii*) Show the goodwill as an asset but amortise it over its useful life. This is the predominant practice. French and Swedish companies often use 10 or 20 years; German companies 15 years.
(*iii*) Write the goodwill off immediately against reserves, thereby never showing an asset and never suffering amortisation charges. This is predominant practice in the UK and Ireland, and is common in the Netherlands and Germany.

8.4 Currency Translation

The Seventh Directive does not include rules relating to foreign currency translation. Consequently, the variety of practice in Europe is even greater for this topic than for other matters connected with consolidation. In the UK, Ireland and the Netherlands there is no law but there are 'standards' on the subject. However, in France and Germany there is no detailed guidance. In Sweden, the guidance from the accountancy body follows Anglo-American practice. In countries where there are no rules on consolidation, practice on translation is obviously varied.

Transactions

Discussion here will begin with the treatment of foreign currency items in an individual company's own accounts. In all countries it is normal to translate assets into local currency once and for all. For example, consider a British company that bought on credit a German computer invoiced in Deutschemarks. In the UK accounts, and assuming no forward purchasing or matching, this asset would normally be frozen into pounds sterling at the date of purchase.

The next matter to consider is the resulting debtors or creditors in such cases. In most countries, if outstanding at a year-end, these amounts would be translated at year-end exchange rates. Thus, there would usually be gains or losses on settlement and at each year-end. However, some German, Swiss and Swedish companies take the conservative approach of recording debtors at the lower of the amounts in German currency at the date of sales and at the year-end. This was discussed in section 6.4.

Long-term liabilities in foreign currencies in an individual company's balance sheet are normally translated at year-end rates.

Losses recognised as a result of the above practices are generally taken immediately into the profit and loss account. However, the treatment of gains is more varied. In the UK gains on both short- and long-term monetary items are taken to profit, even though the gains are unsettled and unrealised. In the Netherlands, short-term gains are taken, but long-term gains are not always. In France, gains are not recognised for individual company accounts and for tax, but can be for consolidated accounts:

GAINS ON MONETARY ITEMS (France, Total Oil)

'Monetary assets and liabilities of the French companies denominated in foreign currencies are translated at the exchange rates ruling on 31 December. The resulting gains or losses are dealt with in the profit and loss account. Consequently the exchange difference accounts arising through the application of the French Revised Chart of Accounts are eliminated.'

In Germany, such gains are not recognised in individual or in group accounts.

Translation of Foreign Financial Statements

Companies in most countries use the current rate method for the translation of the accounts of foreign subsidiaries. This involves:

(*i*) balance sheets translated at year-end rates,
(*ii*) profit and loss accounts translated at average rates for the year,
(*ii*) differences on translation put to reserves.

In the UK, SSAP 20 allows, and many companies use, the closing rate for profit and loss accounts.

In general, continental companies use the average rate for the profit and loss account (see, for example, Switzerland in Table 8.5, France in Tables 8.6 and 8.7, and Germany in Table 8.8). However, the treatment of exchange differences is not always uniform: note the treatment by Total Oil in Table 8.6 but the Anglo-American treatment by Bull in Table 8.7.

The major difference in Europe is in the differential use of the temporal method. This method, which used to be the standard US method in SFAS 8 from 1975 to 1981, requires the use of exchange rates that are appropriate to the valuation basis of the item to be translated. For example, fixed assets (and depreciation charges on them) and stocks held at historical cost are translated at the appropriate historical rates; most profit and loss account items can normally be translated at average rates; cash and debtors are translated at year-end rates.

In the UK SSAP 20 calls for the use of the temporal method for very closely held subsidiaries. In practice its use is very rare. SSAP 20 would call

Table 8.5 Swiss Currency Translation (Adia)

'The accounts of foreign Group companies are translated into Swiss francs according to the following rules: the profit and loss account items are translated by applying

- the annual average exchange rates (weighted in accordance with the monthly sales in the respective currencies) for sales and all other items of the profit and loss account, except the net profit figure;
- the actual exchange rates for the net profit of the year if already transferred;
- the average exchange rates for the month of December for the profit of the year if not yet transferred.

The differences arising from using the various exchange rates are grouped under the heading 'Non-operating income' in the consolidated profit and loss account. Balance sheet items are translated at the average exchange rates for the month of December.'

Table 8.6 French Currency Translation (Total Oil)

Foreign company balance sheets are converted into French francs on the basis of exchange rates at 31 December. This conversion is applied to fixed assets as well as to monetary assets and liabilities. Gains or losses on translation of their balance sheets at the end of the previous year are dealt with:

- in reserves for that part which relates to non-monetary assets (property, plant and equipment, associated companies and trade investments).
- in the profit and loss account for that part which relates to monetary assets (long- and short-term debt and loans and cash balances) and stocks.

Average exchange rates are used for consolidated profit and loss account items so as to approximate to the figures that would be obtained by converting transactions on a daily basis. However, 'Net income' and 'allocations for depreciation and provisions' have been converted, in the same way as balance sheet items, using the rate at 31 December.'

Table 8.7 French Currency Translation (Bull)

'The financial statements of the Group's foreign subsidiaries have been translated into French francs, for consolidation purposes, according to the principles of Statement No 52 of the Financial Accounting Standards Boards of the United States of America. These principles are summarized as follows:

- Assets and liabilities, including accumulated depreciation, are translated at year-end exchange rates.
- Income statement amounts are translated at average monthly rates of exchange.

Gains and losses resulting from translation are accumulated in a separate component of stockholders' equity entitled 'Translation adjustment'. The translation adjustments in 1987 and 1986 are reported on a separate line in the Consolidated Statement of Stockholders' Equity.'

Table 8.8 German Currency Translation (AEG)

'The fixed assets of consolidated foreign affiliates and the book values of the non-consolidated foreign affiliates are translated at the median currency exchange rate in effect at the year-end of the year of acquisition. All other assets, liabilities and equity are translated at the median exchange rate in effect at the end of the current year.

In the statement of income, revenue and expense items are translated at the average exchange rates of the current year. Exceptions are the depreciation of fixed assets and gains and losses on the disposal of fixed and financial assets, which are translated at the rates in effect at acquisition. Foreign affiliates' profits and losses for the year are translated at the median exchange rate in effect at the balance sheet date. The difference arising from translating at the average rate for the year and the rate in effect at year-end is included under other operating income or expenses.'

for differences on translation to be taken to the profit and loss account, as SFAS 8 used to require. The temporal method is rare in the Netherlands. In France, the closing rate and the temporal method are allowed, although the former is more common. The main exponents of the temporal method now are a number of German-based multinationals. They do not all take translation differences to reserves (see Table 8.9). Furthermore, the use of the temporal method is sometimes approximate; for example; some companies use the rates of the year-end of acquisition of an asset rather than the day of acquisition (again, see Table 8.9). Assuming that the Deutschemark is usually strong against currencies of subsidiaries, use of the temporal method will raise fixed asset values compared to use of closing rates of exchange, and depreciation charges will also be higher.

8.5 Segmental Reporting

The EC Directives require turnover to be split by sector and market. This latter requirement can be found in the laws that have implemented the Directives. In the UK, the practice of most large companies goes further because the Companies Act 1985 requires pre-tax profit to be shown by sector. Further, in 1990, SSAP 25 was issued which requires disclosure of turnover, pre-tax profit and capital employed, by both sector and market. This approximates to US practice.

In general, practice in continental Europe does not go beyond that required by the rules implemented as a result of the Directive; and segmental reporting is not standard practice outside the EC.

CHAPTER 9

Conclusions

Financial reporting in Europe differs internationally for long-run, deep-seated reasons. However, as globalisation of the securities markets progresses and as the European Community is moulded into a unified market, these accounting differences become obstructions. They make life more difficult for investors, lenders, traders, managers of companies, purchasers of companies, auditors, and so on.

Perhaps the greatest force for the removal of differences is commercial pressure. This probably explains the large number of annual reports from major continental European companies that are translated into English (often American English) and the widespread adoption of Anglo-American techniques such as the equity method of consolidation and lease capitalisation. However, this pressure operates selectively and without precision.

The EC Commission began to be an important force for accounting harmonisation in the late 1970s, with the effects being particularly noticeable by the late 1980s. Once the Seventh Directive has been implemented throughout the EC, a considerable degree of harmonisation will have been achieved compared to the situation in 1980. Nevertheless, many areas of practice are still very varied within the EC: fixed asset valuation, lease accounting, funds flow statements, currency translation. Eventually, more harmonisation will be achieved by commercial pressure and by EC Directives, but important differences will probably survive beyond the 1990s. This leaves investors, lenders, managers, auditors, analysts, etc with major problems of interpretation. These problems are compounded by language difficulties, upon which there are no current EC Directives but a considerable commercial pressure on some companies to use English.

In order to assist in the solution of these problems, this book has tried to lay bare the causes and nature of the international differences, and to analyse the harmonisation process. There is also a Glossary as Appendix III to help with some language difficulties. A further way of assistance is to summarise the main differences in the calculation of net assets and earnings. Most ratios depend on these latter two aggregates or figures that can be derived from them.

In Germany the Association of Investment Analysts (*Deutsche Vereinigung für Finanzanalyse und Anlageberatung*, DVFA) tries to adjust for the discretionary items in German accounts. Its objective is particularly to adjust earnings, not to a UK benchmark of course, but to a more comparable German basis. The rules were rearranged in 1987 as a result of the

*Table 9.1 DVFA Earnings Calculation**

Adjust for:	extraordinary (*ausserordentliche*) exceptional (*ungewöhnliche*) optional (*dispositionsbedingte*)
Detailed adjustments:	start up expenses not to be capitalised no goodwill amortisation no special tax-deductible depreciation no adjustments to special items with reserve character no gains or losses on exceptional, rare or significant disposal of fixed assets grants to be credited over life of asset no temporary amortisation of investments inventories to include production overheads no large transfers to or from inventory or debtor reserves no tax-based write downs no changes to basis of pension provisions no expense equalisation accruals no translation differences on assets and liabilities no disasters no changes in policies no sale of major divisions

* *Ergebnis nach DVFA/SG*, W. Busse von Colbe, K. Geiger, H. Haase, H. Reinhard and G. Schmitt, Schäffer Verlag, 1991.

implementation of the Fourth and Seventh Directives. Some of the main adjustments to German published net profit figures are:

(*i*) exclusion of all extraordinary and prior year items (even gains and losses on the sale of fixed assets which would be 'exceptional items' in the UK);
(*ii*) elimination of excess depreciation due to tax rules or for other reasons;
(*iii*) removal of the effects of changes to long-term provisions which are largely discretionary;
(*iv*) elimination of currency gains and losses on non-trading activities.

The DVFA procedure is outlined in more detail in Table 9.1. In the UK, in 1993, the Institute for Investment Management and Research (IIMR) published the scheme shown in Table 9.2 to establish 'headline earnings'. This is designed to assist with the prediction of future profits or cash flows by eliminating unusual items that are not expected to recur. In both the DVFA and IIMR cases, estimates are still necessary if analysts from outside the company do the calculations. However, in the UK, the system is so well accepted that the *Financial Times* and Extel quote 'headline earnings' figures.

It should be stressed that neither of these methods is attempting to adjust for *international* differences. This is the next stage, which brings with it the major difficulties of adjusting for such items as discussed in this chapter. However, the DVFA and IIMR schemes provide a model for how international adjustments might be made: on a line-by-line basis and using a fixed benchmark towards which to adjust.

Table 9.2 Items to be Excluded or Included in the IIMR's Definition of Headline Earnings

Item	**Out or In**
Profit or losses on the sale or termination of an operation	Out
Profits or losses on the disposal (including expropriation) of fixed assets	Out
Amortisation of goodwill	Out
Costs of reorganising or restructuring having a material effect on the nature and focus of the reporting entity's continuing operations	In
Costs of non-fundamental reorganisation	In
Abortive bid costs	In
Bid defence costs	Out
One-off costs of complying with major new legislation	In
Litigation costs (whether a hazard of normal business or abnormal)	In
Diminution in value of fixed assets	Out
Diminution in value of current assets	In
Profit or loss on capital reorganisation of long term debt	Out
One-off charge or credit relating to a pension fund deficiency or surplus	In
Profits or losses on disposal of trade investments	Out
Profits or losses on disposal of investments held for resale	In

It is probable that most readers of this book will find a UK or US benchmark the most useful, not least because the numbers of listed companies is far greater in each of these two countries than in any continental European country. This chapter concentrates on a benchmark which is a version of UK practice. If a US benchmark is preferred, it will merely be necessary to be mindful of Anglo-American differences, as explained in the companion volume *Interpreting US Financial Statements*, Chapter 7.

Let us start with a reminder of the differences examined in earlier chapters. Table 9.3 above contains the headings of Chapter 2 and some other major areas discussed elsewhere. A further reminder of differences is the classification of European countries shown in Table 3.3. All European countries except for the UK, Ireland, Denmark and the Netherlands are shown there in the 'macro' group. For accounts from these countries, the following are some of the adjustments that may be necessary:

Table 9.3 Some Main Areas of International Differences in Financial Reporting

1 Fairness
2 Taxation
3 Conservatism and Accruals
4 Provisions and Reserves
5 Valuation Bases
6 Consolidation
7 Uniformity and Accounting Plans
8 Shareholder Orientation of Financial Statements
9 Publication and Audit
10 Terminology
11 Formats

Action

1 Conservatism	INCREASE net asset values
2 Historical cost	INCREASE net asset values
3 LIFO	INCREASE inventory values for some
4 Translation	EXTRACT translation adjustments from German and other users of the 'temporal' method
5 Consolidation	BEWARE lack of consolidation
6 Associated Companies	INCREASE net assets and profit in cases of non-use of equity method
7 R and D	UK unusual in allowing capitalisation
8 Leases	INCREASE fixed assets and liabilities where leases are not capitalised
9 Pensions	EXAMINE carefully. EXTRACT any pension provisions from shareholders' funds.
10 Provisions	INCREASE shareholders' funds by portion of general provisions
11 Tax	DECREASE depreciation where caused by tax

From the above suggestions, an analyst could construct a detailed benchmark for international comparisons of earnings and net assets.

As a final illustration of the scale of difference, the revelations of Daimler-Benz in 1993 are instructive. For example, for the first half of 1993, results under German rules were a profit of DM 168 m. By contrast, the company published figures under US rules showing a loss of DM 949 m for the same period. Not only is this an astonishingly large difference, but it is also in the opposite direction to that predictable under the conventional view of prudent German accounting. A major reason for the difference is the reversal of provisions which has been a feature of the difficult years of the early 1990s. At the very least, this provides a clear warning that international comparisons of unadjusted reported profits may lead to seriously wrong decisions.

In summary, it is likely to remain impossible for many years to achieve precise comparisons of earnings or net assets figures across Europe. However, this does not mean that users of financial statements should just give up and pretend that all companies are using the same rules. Approximate adjustments and informed questions will lead to better decision-making.

Appendices

APPENDIX I

Extract from the Annual Report of Total Oil, 1992

AUDITORS' REPORT

1992

Ladies and Gentlemen,

In accordance with our appointment we present our report on:

- the audit of the consolidated financial statements of TOTAL which are attached to this report,
- the verifications of the Management Report

relating to the year ended December 31, 1992.

1. OPINION ON THE CONSOLIDATED FINANCIAL STATEMENTS

We have audited the consolidated financial statements by carrying out such procedures as we considered necessary in accordance with the standards of the profession.

We certify that the consolidated financial statements comply with the legal requirements and give a true and fair view of the assets, the financial position and the results of the companies included in the consolidation.

2. SPECIFIC VERIFICATIONS

We have performed specific examinations procedures as required by law, in accordance with the standards of the profession.

We are satisfied that the information included in the management report is fairly presented and is consistent with the consolidated financial statements.

Paris, March 31, 1993

The Statutory Auditors
CABINET CAUVIN, ANGLEYS, SAINT-PIERRE INTERNATIONAL
R. Amirkhanian
F. Angleys

FRINAULT FIDUCIAIRE,
G. Barthes de Ruyter
P. Macioce

ARTHUR ANDERSEN & CO
(An Illinois, USA, Partnership)

(Literal translation from French)

CONSOLIDATED STATEMENT OF INCOME

Total and Subsidiaries

Year ended December 31,	1992	1991
(Amounts in millions of French Francs)		
Sales (Notes 20 and 21)	136,608	143,019
Operating expenses	(125,063)	(128,249)
Depreciation, depletion and amortization of tangible assets	(4,674)	(4,988)
OPERATING INCOME: (Note 20)		
Corporate	(445)	(550)
Business Segments	7,316	10,332
Total operating income	6,871	9,782
Interest income (expense) (Note 22)	(747)	(606)
Dividends on preferred shares of consolidated subsidiaries (Note 14)	(47)	(78)
Other income (expense) (Note 23)	(155)	(809)
Non-recurring items (Note 24)	(539)	(288)
Provisions for income taxes (Note 25)	(1,734)	(1,799)
Equity in income of unconsolidated companies (Note 6)	(1)	71
INCOME BEFORE AMORTIZATION OF ACQUISITION GOODWILL	3,648	6,273
Amortization of acquisition goodwill (Note 26)	(585)	(431)
CONSOLIDATED NET INCOME	3,063	5,842
Minority interest	(216)	(32)
NET INCOME	2,847	5,810
EARNINGS PER SHARE (in French Francs)	13.5	27.5

CONSOLIDATED BALANCE SHEET

Total and Subsidiaries

December, 31	1992	1991
ASSETS		
(Amounts in millions of French Francs)		
FIXED AND OTHER NONCURRENT ASSETS:		
Intangible assets (Note 4)	11,602	10,911
Less: accumulated depreciation and amortization (Note 4)	(2,821)	(2,207)
Intangible assets (Note 4)	8,781	8,704
Property, plant and equipment (Note 5)	84,398	82,005
Less: accumulated depreciation, depletion and amortization (Note 5)	(43,934)	(44,187)
Property, plant and equipment (Note 5)	40,464	37,818
Investments and other non current assets:		
Equity in unconsolidated companies (Note 6)	1,744	1,239
Other investments (Note 7)	4,963	4,795
Other long-term financial assets (Note 8)	5,851	4,765
Investments and other non current assets	12,558	10,799
Total fixed and other non current assets	61,803	57,321
CURRENT ASSETS:		
Inventories (Note 9)	12,927	12,918
Accounts and notes receivable (Note 10)	17,833	18,930
Prepaid expenses and other current assets (Note 11)	7,259	6,839
Marketable securities (Note 12)	517	1,831
Cash and cash equivalents	15,261	16,216
Total current assets	53,797	56,734
TOTAL ASSETS	**115,600**	**114,055**

CONSOLIDATED BALANCE SHEETS

Total and Subsidiaries

December, 31	1992	1991
LIABILITIES AND SHAREHOLDERS' EQUITY		
(Amounts in millions of French Francs)		
SHAREHOLDERS' EQUITY (Note 13):		
Common shares	9,500	2,310
Paid-in surplus	2,582	8,771
Retained earnings	29,299	27,892
Revaluation reserve	718	741
Cumulative translation adjustment	(1,296)	(1,151)
Perpetual subordinated securities repayable in shares (TSDIRAs)	3,864	4,181
Total shareholders' equity	44,667	42,744
REDEEMABLE PREFERRED SHARES ISSUED BY CONSOLIDATED SUBSIDIARIES (Note 14)	1,441	1,364
MINORITY INTEREST	2,273	2,430
LONG-TERM LIABILITIES:		
Reserve for crude oil price changes (Note 15)	198	115
Deferred income taxes	3,354	3,253
Reserve for retirement benefits, pension plans and special termination plans (Note 16)	3,947	3,909
Other liabilities (Note 17)	4,077	5,100
Total long-term liabilities	11,576	12,377
LONG-TERM DEBT:		
Loans (Note 18)	20,247	17,320
Deposits	406	755
Total long-term debt	20,653	18,075
CURRENT LIABILITIES:		
Accounts and notes payable	14,105	14,590
Other creditors and accrued liabilities (Note 19)	11,335	12,344
Current portion of long-term debt	2,644	2,248
Short-term borrowings	4,653	6,155
Bank overdrafts	2,253	1,728
Total current liabilities	34,990	37,065
TOTAL LIABILITIES AND SHAREHOLDERS' EQUITY	**115,600**	**114,055**

CONSOLIDATED STATEMENTS OF CHANGES IN SHAREHOLDERS' EQUITY

Total and Subsidiaries

	Common shares issued		Paid in surplus	Retained earnings	Revaluation reserve	Cumulative translation adjustments	TSDIRAs	Shareholders' equity
	Number	Amount						
(Amounts in millions of French francs)								
AS OF JANUARY 1, 1991	36,639,422	1,832	3,040	21,818	752	(1,003)	6,685	33,124
Cash dividend (FF 23 per share and FF 11.50 per TSDIRA) (1)	—	—	—	(936)	—	—	—	(936)
Net income	—	—	—	5,810	—	—	—	5,810
Issuance of common shares	9,564,007	478	5,731	1,200	—	—	(2,504)	4,905
Change in revaluation reserve	—	—	—	—	(11)	—	—	(11)
Translation adjustment	—	—	—	—	—	(148)	—	(148)
AS OF DECEMBER 31, 1991	46,203,429	2,310	8,771	27,892	741	(1,151)	4,181	42,744
Four-for-one stock split	138,610,287	6,930	(6,930)	—	—	—	—	—
Cash dividend (FF 7per share and FF 28 per TSDIRA)	—	—	—	(1,440)	—	—	—	(1,440)
Net income	—	—	—	2,847	—	—	—	2,847
Issuance of common shares	3,520,740	177	502	—	—	—	—	679
Change in revaluation reserve	—	—	5	—	(23)	—	—	(18)
Translation adjustment	—	—	—	—	—	(145)	—	(145)
Conversion of TSDIRAs into common shares	1,668,504	83	234	—	—	—	(317)	—
AS OF DECEMBER 31, 1992	**190,002,960**	**9,500**	**2,582**	**29,299**	**718**	**(1,296)**	**3,864**	**44,667**

(1) For 1990, the dividend on TSDIRAs paid in 1991 was equal to one-half of the dividend paid on common shares.

CONSOLIDATED STATEMENTS OF CASH FLOWS

Total and Subsidiaries (Note 34)

Year ended December 31,	1992	1991
(Amounts in millions of French Francs)		
CASH FLOWS FROM OPERATING ACTIVITIES		
Net income	2,847	5,810
Minority interest	216	32
Depreciation, depletion and amortization	5,449	6,180
Long-term liabilities and valuation allowances	663	755
Unsuccessful exploration costs	777	877
Funds generated from operations	9,952	13,654
Cost-oil reimbursed on production sharing contracts	551	614
Reserve for crude oil price changes	101	(1,844)
(Gains) Losses on sales of fixed assets	(14)	(400)
Dividends on preferred shares of consolidated subsidiaries	47	72
Dividends less than equity in income of unconsolidated companies	32	(59)
Decrease (increase) in working capital:		
Inventories	(248)	2,382
Accounts and notes receivable	791	2,198
Prepaid expenses and other current assets	256	(213)
Accounts and notes payable	(785)	(678)
Other creditors and accrued liabilities	(662)	(1,064)
Adjustment for companies acquired or sold on current accounts excluding inventories	—	(10)
Other	(160)	22
CASH FLOWS FROM OPERATING ACTIVITIES	9,861	14,674
CASH FLOWS FROM INVESTING ACTIVITIES		
Increase in tangible and intangible assets	(10,468)	(9,584)
Increase in equity investments	(389)	(1,104)
Exploration costs directly charged to expenses	(627)	(766)
Payment for major purchases of consolidated subsidiaries, net of cash acquired	(1,133)	(1,167)
Increase in long-term loans granted	(2,219)	(1,835)
Proceeds from disposal of fixed assets	1,185	1,610
Repayment of long-term loans granted	337	634
(Increase) and buyout of minority interest	(197)	(32)
Decrease (increase) in marketable securities	1,316	(258)
CASH FLOWS FROM INVESTING ACTIVITIES	(12,195)	(12,502)
CASH FLOWS FROM FINANCING ACTIVITIES		
Proceeds from issuance of shares:		
Parent company's shareholders	679	2,738
Minority shareholders	86	63
Dividends paid:		
Parent company's shareholders and holders of TSDIRAs	(1,440)	(936)
Minority shareholders	(191)	(219)
Dividends on preferred shares of consolidated subsidiaries	(47)	(72)
Net increase (decrease) in long-term debt	5,591	3,929
Increase (decrease) in short-term borrowings and bank overdrafts	(3,227)	(2,190)
CASH FLOWS FROM FINANCING ACTIVITIES	1,451	3,313
NET INCREASE (DECREASE) IN CASH AND CASH EQUIVALENTS	(883)	5,485
Effect of exchange rate and changes in reporting entity on cash and cash equivalents	(72)	(177)
Cash and cash equivalents at the beginning of period	16,216	10,908
CASH AND CASH EQUIVALENTS AT THE END OF THE YEAR	15,261	16,216
SUPPLEMENTAL DISCLOSURES OF CASH FLOW INFORMATION		
Cash paid during the year for:		
• Interest (net of amount capitalized)	2,055	2,363
• Income taxes	843	2,032

NOTES TO CONSOLIDATED FINANCIAL STATEMENTS

Total and Subsidiaries

(Amounts in millions of French Francs "MFF")

1. ACCOUNTING POLICIES

The consolidated financial statements of TOTAL and its subsidiaries, together the "Company", have been prepared in accordance with the accounting principles issued by the International Accounting Standards Committee (IASC) and the French law of January 3, 1985.

The financial statements of the consolidated subsidiaries, when prepared in accordance with different accounting principles generally accepted in their country of origin, have been restated accordingly.

All material intercompany accounts, transactions and income have been eliminated.

A) PRINCIPLES OF CONSOLIDATION

Fully consolidated companies are those for which the Company's ownership interest is at least 50% and for which the Company's investment (or loans and advances) is regarded as significant.

Companies in which ownership interest is less than 50%, but over which the Company maintains effective control, are also consolidated.

The Company's interests in oil industry related joint ventures are proportionately consolidated.

Companies in which the percentage of ownership interest equals or exceeds 20% but is less than 50% and for which the Company's investment is regarded as significant are accounted for by the equity method. Under this method, the investment represents the Company's share of the underlying equity of the investee (including income or loss for the period) and is reflected in the consolidated balance sheets as "Equity in unconsolidated companies".

The Company's share of the income or loss of its equity investees is reflected in the consolidated statements of income as "Equity in income of unconsolidated companies".

B) FOREIGN CURRENCY TRANSLATION

(I) Monetary Transactions

Transactions denominated in foreign currencies are translated at the exchange rate prevailing when the transaction is realized. Gains and losses resulting from translation of the balance sheet values of these transactions at the exchange rates prevailing at the end of the period are recorded in "Other income (expense)" in the consolidated statement of income. When a foreign currency loan is specifically contracted to protect a net investment in a foreign consolidated subsidiary or equity investee from the effect of exchange rates fluctuations, the resulting translation differences are recorded in the shareholders' equity in "Cumulative translation adjustment".

(II) Translation of Financial Statements Denominated in Foreign Currencies

The balance sheets of consolidated subsidiaries or equity investees are translated into French francs on the basis of exchange rates at the end of the period. Effective January 1, 1992, the statement of income and the cash flows statement have been translated using the average rate of the period. Foreign exchange differences resulting from such translation are recorded as follows:

- for the Company's share, as "Cumulative translation adjustment" in the shareholder's equity,
- for the minority share, as "Minority interest".

In 1991, net income, depreciation, depletion and amortization expenses and valuation allowances were translated at exchange rates prevailing at the end of the period; other income statement items were translated at the average exchange rates in effect during the period. The effects of differences between exchange rates prevailing at the end of the period and average exchange rates during the period were included in "Other income (expense)".

The impact of this change on the 1991 net income is not material.

C) FINANCIAL INSTRUMENTS

(I) Interest rate and Foreign Currency Agreements

Changes in the market value of interest rate futures, options, caps and floors are recognized as gains or losses in the period of the change. However, when the contracts qualify as hedges, gains and losses on such contracts are recognized in income in the same period as the gains or losses on the item being hedged.

The Company enters into interest rate and foreign currency swap agreements to reduce its exposure to interest rate and foreign currency changes. The differential to be paid or received under such swaps is recognized in income over the life of the related agreements.

(II) Commodity Transactions

The Company uses hedging strategies to help moderate its exposure to fluctuations of crude oil and related products prices. In this case, gains and losses on these contracts are recognized or accrued as a component of the related transactions. When the Company uses such transactions to hedge a portion of its crude oil or petroleum products inventories, gains or losses on such agreements are included in the inventory cost.

Contracts which do not qualify as specific hedges are recorded as follows:

- Forward contracts: unrealized losses are recognized currently while unrealized gains are deferred until the contract is closed out;
- Futures contracts: unrealized gains and losses are recognized in the statement of income currently.

D) INTANGIBLE ASSETS

Acquisition goodwill is amortized on a straight-line basis over periods not exceeding 30 years.

E) PROPERTY, PLANT AND EQUIPMENT

(I) Oil and Gas Exploration and Producing Properties

The Company applies the successful efforts method of accounting for its oil and gas exploration and producing properties (Financial Accounting Standard n° 19) as follows:

- Costs of acquiring unproved properties are capitalized and impairment is made in absence of commercial discovery. Geological and geophysical costs are expensed as incurred. Costs of exploratory dry holes are expensed as the wells are determined to be dry. Drillings in progress and wells where proved reserves have been discovered are capitalized.
- The costs of productive leaseholds and other capitalized costs related to producing activities including tangible and intangible costs are depreciated on the unit-of-production basis using the estimated proved reserves.

Limitation of Net Value of Capitalized Costs A provision for impairment is recognized on a country-by-country basis to the extent net capitalized costs related to proved oil and gas properties exceed the estimated future net cash flows related to such properties.

Production Sharing Contracts The Company conducts oil and gas exploration and development with certain national oil companies under production sharing contracts which entitle the Company to a contractual portion of the oil and gas production to reimburse its operating and exploration and development costs (cost oil). In addition, the Company is generally entitled to share a portion of the net oil and gas revenues subject to the contract (profit oil).

If no successful discovery is achieved, costs incurred are fully reserved since expenditures relating to production sharing contracts are not eligible for reimbursement (dry holes, noncommercial exploration results). In case of subsequent discovery, any impairment previously recorded is revised based on the Company's estimates of future net revenues.

Exploration and production expenses incurred under these agreements that are subject to reimbursement are carried under "Other long-term financial assets".

(II) Other Property, Plant and Equipment

Other property, plant and equipment are carried at cost with the exception of assets that have been acquired before 1976 whose cost has been revalued following the French regulations by the French companies in their own financial statements and for foreign companies, in addition to their own accounts. The revaluation adjustment is maintained at consolidated level and included in shareholders' equity in "Revaluation reserve". This surplus is credited to income over the useful life of the related depreciable fixed assets using their corresponding rates of depreciation, depletion and amortization or upon disposal of the revalued assets.

Fixed assets of significant value which are held under hire purchase and similar agreements are capitalized and depreciated using straight line method. The corresponding commitment is recorded as a liability.

Assets and capitalized leases are depreciated using a straight-line basis over their estimated useful life, as follows:

	Years of estimated useful life
Transportation equipment	5-15
Machinery, plant and equipment:	
• Machinery, installations and tools	5-10
• Furniture and fixtures	5-10
• Refineries:	
Units	8-10
Storage tanks	10-15
Pipelines and related equipment	10-15
Buildings	20-50
Gas infrastructure and distribution facilities	5-10

Equipment subsidies granted by various governments or tax authorities in connection with purchases of fixed assets are deducted from the cost of the related expenditures.

Maintenance and repair costs are charged to income as incurred.

F) OTHER INVESTMENTS

Investments in companies that are less than 20% owned or are excluded from consolidation after consideration of their materiality to the Company's operations are valued at acquisition cost less allowance for impairment in value.

Certain investments were revalued in accordance with the regulations described in paragraph E (ii).

G) INVENTORIES

Inventories are stated at the lower of cost or market value. Cost is determined on a first-in, first-out basis for crude oil and petroleum products inventories. Refined petroleum products inventories of the French subsidiary Total Raffinage Distribution (TRD) were stated at the weighted average cost until December 31, 1991. The effect of changing method for 1992 is a MFF 162 expense. Cost of the other inventories are generally determined on a weighted average basis.

H) OPERATING EXPENSES AND RESERVE FOR CRUDE OIL PRICE CHANGES

The Group net income is presented on an economic approach basis at replacement cost. Instead of the method based on consumption value of petroleum inventories (crude oil and refined products) calculated month-by-month at historical cost (FIFO or weighted production cost), a replacement value method has been computed, based on the cost of the crude oil and refined products over the period considered.

When inventories of crude oil and petroleum products are consumed, the difference between replacement value and historical cost value is defined as the stock effect. When this effect is positive, a reserve for crude oil price changes is made and is charged against income. This reserve is included in the long-term liabilities. When the stock effect is negative, the amount of the reserve for crude oil price changes recorded at opening balance is written back and decreases operating expenses in the income statement.

I) MARKETABLE SECURITIES

Marketable securities are valued at the lower of cost or market value.

J) SITE RESTORATION

The Company provides for estimated major site restoration costs on a unit-of-production basis. Estimated costs are included in "Other liabilities".

K) DEFERRED TAXES

Deferred taxation is provided under the liability method using the latest updated rates of taxation to take into account:

- timing differences in tax charges which arise as a result of variations between taxable income and accounting income of consolidated companies;
- restatements of company financial statements on consolidation.

L) SALES, COSTS AND EXPENSES

Sales are primarily recorded as products are shipped and services are rendered.

Sales are presented net of excise taxes of MFF 34,826 in 1992 and MFF 31,975 in 1991.

Taxes paid in Middle East producing countries are included in the operating costs for MFF 6,496 in 1992 and MFF 7,573 in 1991.

Costs and expenses are charged to income in the period in which the related sales are recognized.

M) ACCOUNTING FOR EMPLOYEES SHARE SUBSCRIPTION AND SHARE PURCHASE PLANS - DEFERRED COMPENSATION

The Company generally grants to its employees a discount from the market price for shares purchased pursuant to share subscription and share purchase plans. A liability is recorded for this discount, measured at the date of grant. The cost of this deferred compensation to employees is spread over the period of time between the date of grant and the date on which the grantee may first exercise the option.

N) RESEARCH AND DEVELOPMENT EXPENSES

The expenses for research and development are charged to income as incurred.

The total of such costs expensed for the years ended December 31, 1992 and 1991 were MFF 978 and MFF 968.

O) INTEREST EXPENSE

Interest charges relating to the direct financing of major projects under construction, including development works on oil and gas properties, are capitalized. All other interest is expensed currently.

P) CONSOLIDATED STATEMENT OF CASH FLOWS

The consolidated statement of cash flows is included in the consolidated financial statements for 1992 in replacement of the consolidated statement of changes in financial position presented in 1991. The Company applies principles stated in the US Standard n° 95 of the Financial Accounting Standard Board (FASB).

2. CHANGES IN GROUP STRUCTURE AND SUBSEQUENT EVENTS

A) CHANGES IN GROUP STRUCTURE

Yacco On January 14, 1992, the Company acquired 100% of Yacco, a French company that produces and markets high quality lubricants for the automotive industry.

Polichem In February 1992, the Company acquired from the Italian group Varasi 60% of Polichem group, specialized in printing inks in Italy.

In July 1992, the Company swapped 22% of Coates Lorilleux Italiana against 18% of Polichem SA with the Italian group Polifin.

Petrogal On May 22, 1992, a holding company "Petrocontrol" formed by TOTAL and several Portuguese industry and finance investors acquired 25% of Petrogal. The share of the Company in the capital of Petrocontrol is 48%.

The acquisition cost net of cash acquired amounts for these companies to MFF 1,133.

B) SUBSEQUENT EVENTS

Sale of Total Canada Oil & Gas Ltd In February 1993, the Company sold its entire 53% stake in Total Canada Oil & Gas representing 18,794,695 shares at a unit price of Canadian dollars 9.75.

3. CONSOLIDATED SUBSIDIARIES

As of December 31, 1992, 316 subsidiaries were consolidated of which 282 are fully consolidated, 4 are consolidated by the proportional method and 30 are accounted for on the equity basis.

		Company's share%
EXPLORATION - PRODUCTION		
	Total Exploration	100.0
	Total Oil Marine	100.0
	Total Norge	100.0
	Total Oil & Gas Nederland	100.0
	Total Mineraria Oil & Gas	100.0
	Compagnie Française des Pétroles (Algérie)	100.0
	Total Algérie	100.0
	Total Yemen	99.8
	Total Syrie	99.8
	Total Exploration Production Cameroun (Tepcam)	79.0
	Total Angola	100.0
	Tepma Colombie	100.0
	Total Indonésie	100.0
	Total Thaïlande	100.0
	Total Myanmar Exploration Production	99.8
	Total Austral	99.8
	Ranchmen's Resources Ltd	52.3
	Total Oil & Gas Canada	53.2
	Total Exploration Production Russie	99.8
TRADING / MIDDLE EAST		
	Total Transport Maritime	99.7
	Total Transport Corporation	100.0
	Total International Ltd	100.0
	Total Abu Al Bu Khoosh	99.7
	Total Qatar Oil & Gas	99.8
REFINING - MARKETING		
	Total Raffinage Distribution	99.8
	Totalgaz	99.8
	Stela	99.7
	Les Fils Charvet	96.6
	Soft SA	98.8
	Yacco	98.7
	Compagnie Pétrolière de l'Est	99.7
	Pro SNC	99.1
	La Francilienne de Confort	99.7
	Distributeurs de Combustibles Associés	99.3
	Total Solvants	99.7
	Total Deutschland	100.0
	Total Hungaria	75.0
	Total Austria	70.0
	Total Italia	100.0
	Air Total International	99.0
	Total Oil (Great Britain) Ltd	100.0
P	Lindsey Oil Refinery	50.0
	Total Belgique Luxembourg	100.0

		Company's share%
REFINING - MARKETING		
	Total Nederland	100.0
P	Total Raffinaderij Nederland	55.0
	Total Espana	100.0
	Total Outre-mer	100.0
	Total Sénégal	86.6
	Total Côte d'Ivoire	76.6
	Total Turkiye	51.0
	Total Nigeria	60.0
	Total Kenya	78.6
	Total South Africa Pty	57.6
	Total Petroleum (North America) (pre-consolidated)	54.0
CHEMICALS		
	Total Chimie	100.0
	Hutchinson (pre-consolidated) (a)	99.8
	La Seigneurie (pre-consolidated)	99.8
	Peintures Avi	99.9
	Cie Financière de Peintures (Cofidep)	99.2
	Sté Languedocienne de Micron-Couleurs	100.0
	Sté Nantaise des Encres	100.0
	Bostik SA (France)	99.9
	Coates Lorilleux SA	100.0
	Bostik Holding Nederland	100.0
	Cray Valley SA	100.0
	Polichem	77.6
	Coates Brothers PLC	100.0
	Total Coatings	100.0
	Total Haering	60.0
	Cray Valley Kunstharze GmbH	100.0
MINING		
	Total Compagnie minière	100.0
	Total Compagnie minière France	100.0
	Total Exploration South Africa	85.1
	Total Minatco Ltd	100.0
CORPORATE AND MULTIPLE ACTIVITIES		
	Total (Parent Company)	100.0
	Société Financière d'Auteuil	99.0
	Omnium de Participations S.A.	99.9
	Omnium Insurance and Reinsurance Cy	100.0
	Total America, Inc. (pre-consolidated)	100.0
	Total Resources Canada Ltd	100.0
	Total Australia Ltd	100.0
	Total Oil Holdings Ltd	100.0
	Total Finance Nederland	100.0

P = Proportionately consolidated
(a) Including Spontex.

4. INTANGIBLE ASSETS

December 31,	1992			1991
	Cost	**Accumulated depreciation and amortization**	**Net**	**Net**
ACQUISITION GOODWILL				
Exploration and production	94	23	71	27
Refining and marketing	2,159	739	1,420	1,415
Chemicals	5,878	769	5,109	5,215
Mining	268	247	21	48
Other	136	63	73	66
TOTAL ACQUISITION GOODWILL	8,535	1,841	6,694	6,771
OTHER INTANGIBLES				
Patents and trademarks	472	190	282	330
Trade agreements	402	228	174	263
Entrance fees	141	58	83	111
Goodwill	989	170	819	747
Other	1,063	334	729	482
TOTAL OTHER INTANGIBLES	3,067	980	2,087	1,933
TOTAL	**11,602**	**2,821**	**8,781**	**8,704**

5. PROPERTY, PLANT AND EQUIPMENT

December 31,	1992			1991
	Cost	**Accumulated depreciation, depletion, and amortization**	**Net**	**Net**
OIL AND GAS EXPLORATION AND PRODUCING PROPERTIES				
• Proved properties	28,021	16,629	11,392	12,761
• Unproved properties	898	343	555	281
• Work in progress	5,716	—	5,716	4,160
TOTAL OIL AND GAS EXPLORATION AND PRODUCING PROPERTIES	34,635	16,972	17,663	17,202
OTHER PROPERTY, PLANT AND EQUIPMENT				
• Transportation equipment	1,320	1,012	308	364
• Machinery, plant and equipment	19,768	14,259	5,509	5,355
• Land	3,439	219	3,220	2,889
• Buildings	11,236	5,186	6,050	5,920
• Construction in progress	2,389	5	2,384	1,375
• Other	11,611	6,281	5,330	4,713
TOTAL OTHER PROPERTY, PLANT AND EQUIPMENT	49,763	26,962	22,801	20,616
TOTAL	**84,398**	**43,934**	**40,464**	**37,818**

Property, plant and equipment presented above include the following amounts for buildings and machinery, plant and equipment leases that have been capitalized:

December 31,	1992			1991
	Cost	Accumulated depreciation, depletion, and amortization	Net	Net
• Machinery, plant and equipment	4,437	3,881	556	798
• Buildings	867	347	520	549
TOTAL	**5,304**	**4,228**	**1,076**	**1,347**

6. EQUITY IN UNCONSOLIDATED COMPANIES

The Company's share in the equity and income or loss of unconsolidated companies is summarized below:

	December 31,				Year ended December 31,	
	1992	1991	1992	1991	1992	1991
	% owned	% owned	Invest-ment	Invest-ment	Equity in income (loss)	Equity in income (loss)
Petrocontrol	48.00	N/A	568	N/A	(75)	N/A
SARA	25.00	25.00	269	243	34	18
Ruwais Fertilizer Industries	33.33	33.33	138	130	—	—
I.P.C.	23.75	23.75	137	157	—	—
Wepec	20.00	20.00	125	128	—	—
Algeco	25.37	25.37	87	81	16	67
Tüpgaz	49.88	49.86	75	78	(2)	—
Autogas Nord	50.00	50.00	69	137	(5)	(10)
Total Maroc	49.99	49.99	66	67	6	11
Cie Européenne des Pétroles	25.00	25.00	48	69	(21)	(26)
ADPC	23.75	23.75	37	(2)	45	4
Cofraland	30.75	30.75	33	36	(3)	(3)
Divers		—	92	115	4	10
TOTAL			**1,744**	**1,239**	**(1)**	**71**

7. OTHER INVESTMENTS

December 31,	1992			1991
	Cost	**Valuation allowance**	**Net**	**Net**
PUBLICLY TRADED EQUITY SECURITIES				
Paribas	769	—	769	769
Compagnie Générale de Géophysique	287	—	287	287
Christian Dior SA	214	—	214	208
Unibail	209	27	182	209
Saga Petroleum	136	—	136	155
Banque Colbert (formerly BAFIP)	72	—	72	47
Financière Agache	52	—	52	52
Other	101	40	61	108
TOTAL PUBLICLY TRADED (a)	**1,840**	**67**	**1,773**	**1,835**

December 31,	1992			1991
	Cost	**Valuation allowance**	**Net**	**Net**
OTHER EQUITY SECURITIES				
Abu Dhabi Gas Industries Ltd	273	—	273	273
Nogat	140	6	134	133
Technip	112	—	112	112
Natref	87	—	87	91
Rossing Uranium Ltd	79	18	61	64
Financière Fougerolle	47	—	47	77
Compagnie privée d'El Rhaba	—	—	—	69
Sonepar Distribution	—	—	—	69
Abu Dhabi Gas Liquefaction Company	39	39	—	7
Other (b)	3,500	1,024	2,476	2,065
TOTAL NON-PUBLICLY TRADED	**4,277**	**1,087**	**3,190**	**2,960**
TOTAL (c)	**6,117**	**1,154**	**4,963**	**4,795**
(a) Market value of publicly traded equity securities			2,089	2,337

(b) Net value of investments excluded from consolidation after considering their materiality to the Company's operations accounts for MFF 1,864 and MFF 1,482 as of December 31, 1992 and 1991, respectively.

(c) As of December 31, 1991, the aggregate cost of the other investments and valuation allowances amounted to MFF 5,623 and MFF 828, respectively.

8. OTHER LONG-TERM FINANCIAL ASSETS

December 31,	1992			1991
	Cost	Valuation allowance	Net	Net
PRODUCTION SHARING CONTRACTS (P.S.C.):				
• Exploration and development costs without proved reserves	1,505	1,460	45	40
• Exploration and development costs on proved reserves	2,608	762	1,846	1,183
Total P.S.C.	4,113	2,222	1,891	1,223
Loans	3,763	444	3,319	2,881
Security deposits	449	1	448	595
Other	194	1	193	66
TOTAL	**8,519**	**2,668**	**5,851**	**4,765**

9. INVENTORIES

December 31,	1992	1991
Crude oil and natural gas	2,602	2,336
Refined petroleum products and products in process	6,358	6,847
Chemical products	2,519	2,618
Coal, uranium and other minerals	337	245
Supplies and other inventories	1,111	872
TOTAL	**12,927**	**12,918**

10. ACCOUNTS AND NOTES RECEIVABLE

December 31,	1992			1991
	Cost	Valuation allowance	Net	Net
Receivables from customers	16,973	777	16,196	17,022
Notes receivable	1,637	—	1,637	1,908
TOTAL	**18,610**	**777**	**17,833**	**18,930**

11. PREPAID EXPENSES AND OTHER CURRENT ASSETS

December 31,	1992			1991
	Cost	Valuation allowance	Net	Net
Advances to suppliers and current accounts	1,962	—	1,962	2,516
Receivables from states (including taxes)	1,990	—	1,990	2,345
Prepayments and accrued income	430	—	430	424
Other	2,982	105	2,877	1,554
TOTAL	**7,364**	**105**	**7,259**	**6,839**

12. MARKETABLE SECURITIES

December 31,	1992		1991	
	Net	Market value	Net	Market value
Publicly traded securities	468	497	1,710	1,719
Non-publicly traded securities	49	—	121	—
TOTAL	**517**		**1,831**	

13. SHAREHOLDERS' EQUITY

A) COMMON SHARES

Change in the Number of Shares On January 27, 1992, the Board of Directors declared, effective February 10, 1992, a four-for-one stock split which was effected through the capitalization of paid-in surplus for an amount equal to the aggregate par value of the additional common shares created. The par value remains at FF 50 per common share.

All information related to the number of shares, share subscription and purchase plans and calculations per share have been restated in this annual report accordingly.

Reduction of the French State's Participation in TOTAL Stock During the summer of 1992, the French State reduced its participation in TOTAL stock by over 26%. The decrease of the French State's ownership was effected through the following operations:

- a global public offering by the French State of 22,900,000 shares in financial markets from June 23, 1992 to June 25, 1992;
- a public exchange offer by the French State of petroleum certificates for TOTAL shares from June 26, 1992 to July 27, 1992. 15,101,420 petroleum certificates were exchanged for 11,326,065 shares;
- direct sale by the French State of 14,296,725 shares to three major institutional investors on July 2, 1992.

Description of the Shares TOTAL shares have a par value of FF 50. The Combined Shareholders' Meeting of December 14, 1992 resolved to eliminate the division of the capital of the Company into two different classes of shares ("A" and "B"). Consequently, there is only one class of shares.

Shares may be held in either bearer or registered form. However, the shares owned by either the French State or a public body or department having a legal existence or by a public limited company in which the State has a direct majority shareholding and which have been designated by the State (that is, all shares which are aggregated for the purposes of exercising the subscription, allotment and voting rights with which the State is credited) must be registered.

The bylaws (charter) of the Company provides that the French State shall have the right to assign its shares as well as the subscription and allotment rights attaching thereto, to any public body or department having a legal existence as well as any public limited company mentioned above. In such a case, such shares are aggregated with the shares held by the State for the purpose of exercising the subscription, allotment and voting rights attached to such shares.

The assignment to any unrelated third parties of shares constituing the aggregated participation of the French State requires the approval of the Board of Directors of TOTAL.

Holders of the Company's shares have a preemptive right to subscribe for additional shares issued by the Company on a pro rata basis according to their respective holding of shares.

Each share confers to its holder the right to one vote at the Shareholders' Meeting.

However, effective from December 14, 1994, all fully paid-up shares registered in the name of the same shareholder for at least two years, and any shares issued to such shareholders without consideration in registered form in connection with any increase in the registered capital of the Company by way of capitalization of reserves, profits or premiums, carry double voting rights. The merger of the Company shall have no impact on such double voting rights, which may be exercised at the meeting of shareholders of the absorbing company if so provided for in the bylaws of such company.

At a Shareholders' Meeting, the number of single voting rights which may be exercised by a shareholder acting on his own behalf or by proxy, with respect to the shares held directly and indirectly and the proxies given to such shareholder, may not exceed 10% of the total number of voting rights attached to the Company's shares. However, should the shareholder possess and/or represent double voting rights, the resulting additional voting rights, and only these, may be exercised in excess of the limit above, provided that the total voting rights exercised by such shareholder shall not exceed 20% of the total voting rights attached to the Company's shares.

The above restrictions become null and void if any individual or entity, acting alone or in cooperation with one or more individuals or entities, holds at least two thirds of the total registered capital of the Company following a public tender offer for all of the Company's shares.

EVOLUTION IN THE OWNERSHIP OF COMMON SHARES

	Number of shares	**% of stock ownership**	**% of voting rights** (1)
DECEMBER 31, 1991			
French State and related shareholders (AGF and GAN) (2)	62,783,800	33.97	38.97
DECEMBER 31, 1992			
French State (*)	11,160,206	5.87	5.91
Groupe des Assurances Nationales (GAN), Assurances Générales de France (AGF), Crédit Lyonnais (3) (*)	18,529,437	9.76	9.81

(1) The total number of voting rights as of December 31, 1992 is 188,867,560, corresponding to 190,002,960 shares minus 1,135,400 shares held by the Company in connection with the share price stabilisation and share purchase plans.
(2) As defined in the bylaws (see above).
(3) Shares subject to the Shareholders' Agreement. The Shareholders' Agreement was signed on June 26, 1992 by the French State, AGF, Crédit Lyonnais and GAN. Through this Agreement, the French State and the three companies agreed to comply with certain rules affecting the holding and transfer of 18,529,437 of TOTAL's shares held by the three companies (SFB announcement n° 92-2503, September 18, 1992).
(*) Shareholders acting in concert with respect to the Shareholders' Agreement as described.

Pursuant to article 356-3 of the French law of July 24, 1966 concerning commercial companies, notice is hereby given that no other known shareholder held 5% or more of the Company's share capital or the voting rights at the end of 1992.

SHARES ISSUED AND OUTSTANDING

	A shares	B shares	TOTAL common shares
AS OF JANUARY 1, 1991	157,703	36,481,719	36,639,422
Issued in connection with:			
• 1979 bonds conversion		163,133	163,133
• Employees share subscription plans		41,971	41,971
• Merger with OFP		2,119,428	2,119,428
• Exercise of warrants to purchase shares		536	536
• Capital increase		3,100,000	3,100,000
• Public exchange offer on Hutchinson		848,631	848,631
• Conversion of perpetual subordinated securities repayable in shares		3,290,308	3,290,308
Conversion of B shares into A shares	41,528	(41,528)	—
AS OF DECEMBER 31, 1991	**199,231**	**46,004,198**	**46,203,429**
Four-for-one stock split	597,693	138,012,594	138,610,287
Issued in connection with:			
• 1979 bonds conversion		422,096	422,096
• Employees share subscription plans		110,392	110,392
• Exercise of warrants to purchase shares		2,988,252	2,988,252
• Conversion of perpetual subordinated securities repayable in shares		1,668,504	1,668,504
Conversion of B shares into A shares (a)	(796,924)	796,924	—
AS OF DECEMBER 31, 1992	—	**190,002,960**	**190,002,960**

(a) The Shareholders' Meeting of December 14, 1992 resolved to eliminate the division of the capital of the Company into two different classes of shares ("A" and "B").

Warrants In connection with the merger of OFP into the Company in 1991, 332,821 outstanding warrants to purchase OFP shares were converted into warrants to purchase common shares of the Company under the following exercise conditions:

- nine shares per warrant,
- exercise price: FF 1,950 (FF 216.67 per share).

Of the 332,586 warrants outstanding as of December 31, 1991, 332,028 have been exercised and 558 have become worthless as of December 31, 1992.

B) PERPETUAL SUBORDINATED SECURITIES REPAYABLE IN SHARES

On June 28, 1990, the Company issued 8,804,204 perpetual subordinated securities repayable in shares ("TSDIRAs") with a par value of FF 761 each for an aggregate par value of FF 6,699,999,244. These securities were subscribed by the French State in connection with the Company's acquisition of assets from the Orkem Group. In the second half of 1990, the French State transferred 854,240 TSDIRAs to Groupe des Assurances Nationales (GAN) and 1,971,000 TSDIRAs to Assurances Générales de France (AGF).

Repayment The duration of TSDIRAs is equal to that of the Company. Each TSDIRA is repayable at the holders' discretion on the basis of four shares of the Company for one TSDIRA on the following terms:

- upon each new issuance of TOTAL shares for cash, the maximum number of shares of the Company that may be obtained in repayment of TSDIRAs is limited to 35/65ths of the number of new shares subscribed by persons other than the French State, after deduction of new shares of the Company effectively subscribed by the French State;
- upon each new issuance of TOTAL shares reserved for investors other than the French State, subscribed in cash or in kind, and upon each new issuance of TOTAL shares resulting from conversion, exchange, repayment, exercise of a warrant or stock option or otherwise subscribed by investors other than the French State, the maximum number of shares of the Company that may be obtained in repayment of the perpetual subordinated securities repayable in shares is limited to 35/65ths of the number of new shares issued.
- In case of liquidation of the Company, the perpetual subordinated securities repayable in shares are repaid for shares.

Any issuance of shares resulting from the conversion of debentures issued in June 1979 is excluded from the aforementioned provisions.

HOLDING OF TSDIRAS	French State	Institutional Investors GAN - AGF	Total outstanding
JUNE 28, 1990	8,804,204	—	8,804,204
Transfers	(2,825,240)	2,825,240	—
Conversion into shares	(19,380)	—	(19,380)
DECEMBER 31, 1990	5,959,584	2,825,240	8,784,824
Conversion into shares	(2,232,130)	(1,058,178)	(3,290,308)
DECEMBER 31, 1991	3,727,454	1,767,062	5,494,516
Conversion into shares	(282,977)	(134,149)	(417,126)
DECEMBER 31, 1992	**3,444,477**	**1,632,913**	**5,077,390**

Dividends The TSDIRAs are entitled to receive an annual dividend equal to four times the net dividend paid on common shares. This dividend is payable each year on the same day that the payment of the dividend on common shares is made.

C) CONVERTIBLE BONDS

In June 1979, the Company issued 1,908,375 convertible bonds with a par value of FF 200 per bond, which were convertible into TOTAL shares. These bonds, listed on the Paris Stock Exchange, bore interest at the following rates:

7.5% from July 1, 1979 through December 31, 1982

8.0% from January 1, 1983 through December 31, 1986

9.0% from January 1, 1987 through December 31, 1991

These bonds came to maturity on January 1, 1992. Of the 110,249 bonds which were outstanding as of December 31, 1991, 104,031 bonds were converted at a rate of 4,04 shares per bond; i.e., into 422,096 shares, after exercise of fractional shares.

After the grace period between January 1, 1992 and March 31, 1992, granted to holders for exercising their rights, the 6,218 bonds which had not been converted were called for reimbursement.

14. REDEEMABLE PREFERRED SHARES ISSUED BY CONSOLIDATED SUBSIDIARIES

These shares are issued by North America consolidated companies, Total Energy Resources Finance, Inc. (TERFIN), Total Energy Capital, Inc. (TECI) in the United States and Ranchmen's Resources in Canada, and carry a dividend which depends upon the rate applicable to class AA commercial paper for the TERFIN and TECI shares or a fixed rate for Ranchmen's. The shares are redeemable at the issuing companies' discretion.

A) CHANGES IN CONSOLIDATED SUBSIDIARIES' REDEEMABLE PREFERRED SHARES

	MFF
JANUARY 1, 1991	1,367
Foreign currency translation effect	14
Conversion of Ranchmen's Resources Ltd redeemable shares into Class "A" non-voting shares	(17)
DECEMBER 31, 1991	1,364
Foreign currency translation effect	80
Conversion of Ranchmen's Resources Ltd redeemable shares into Class "A" non-voting shares	(3)
DECEMBER 31, 1992	1,441

B) DIVIDENDS ON PREFERRED SHARES OF CONSOLIDATED SUBSIDIARIES

Year ended December 31,	1992 MFF	1991 MFF
Redeemable preferred shares issued by:		
TERFIN	15	28
TECI	26	42
Ranchmen's Resources Ltd	6	8
TOTAL	**47**	**78**

15. RESERVE FOR CRUDE OIL PRICE CHANGES

	Group interest	Minority interest	Total
Refining-Marketing France	10	—	10
Refining-Marketing Foreign subsidiaries	73	32	105
AMOUNTS AS OF DECEMBER 31, 1991	**83**	**32**	**115**
ALLOWANCE (WRITE-BACK) OF THE YEAR 1992:			
Refining-Marketing France	(8)	—	(8)
Refining-Marketing Foreign subsidiaries	82	27	109
Impact on the net income 1992	74	27	101
Effect of exchange rates and changes in reporting entity	(15)	(3)	(18)
	59	24	83
Refining-Marketing France	2	—	2
Refining-Marketing Foreign subsidiaries	140	56	196
AMOUNTS AS OF DECEMBER 31, 1992	**142**	**56**	**198**

16. RESERVE FOR RETIREMENT BENEFITS, PENSION PLANS AND SPECIAL SPECIAL TERMINATION PLANS

In accordance with the laws and practices of each country, the Company participates in employee benefit pension plans offering death and disability, retirement and special termination benefits. For defined contribution plans and multi-employer plans, expenses correspond to the contributions paid. For defined benefit pension plans, accruals and prepaid expenses are determined using the Projected Unit Credit method. The Company records accruals and prepaid expenses following the International Accounting Standards (IAS) and in accordance with the prevailing accounting practice in each country.

In the context of its listing on the New York Stock Exchange, the Company discloses the following information in accordance with the US Standards (FAS 87 and 88):

		1992	1991
Vested benefits		5,220	5,037
Non vested benefits		767	782
Accumulated benefit obligation		5,987	5,819
Effect of future salary increases		1,140	1,174
Projected benefit obligation		7,127	6,993
Market value of investments		(3,136)	(2,986)
Funded status		3,991	4,007
Unrecognized transition obligation		(417)	(462)
Unrecognized prior service cost		(90)	(88)
Unrecognized actuarial net gains or losses		(321)	(222)
Net accrued under US Standards		3,163	3,235
including:	Accruals	3,693	3,663
	Prepaid	(530)	(428)

The net accruals accounted in consolidated statements as of December 31, 1992 amount to MFF 3,793. They can be compared to the figures shown under US Standards as follows:

		1992
Net accruals under US Standards		3,163
• Excess funding of plans recognized in income only when paid back to the Company		374
• Impacts of transition obligation, of prior service cost and of actuarial gains recognized with a different timing under local regulations		256
Net accrued in consolidated statements		3,793
including:	Accruals	3,947
	Prepaid	(154)

The cost of defined benefit pension plans calculated following the US Standards is as follows:

	1992	1991
Service cost for the period	209	249
Interest cost	594	585
Return on investment	(305)	(360)
Net amortization and deferral	(19)	113
Exceptional items	37	58
TOTAL COST	516	645

In the statement of income for 1992, the Company records the same total cost despite the differences in the timing of unrecognized items and in the accounting of the excess funding of plans.

Actuarial assumptions have been determined by actuaries on a country by country basis and company by company.

They are included in the following range:

Discount rates	8-10%
Future salary increases	5-10%
Expected long-term return on assets	8-11%
Average residual active live	10-25 years

17. OTHER LIABILITIES

December 31,	1992	1991
Litigation and accrued penalty claims	793	884
Restructuring costs	506	973
Specific sector risks	—	340
Site restoration	795	732
Other	1,983	2,171
TOTAL	**4,077**	**5,100**

18. LONG-TERM DEBT (LOANS)

Long-term loans consist of:

December 31,	1992			1991		
	Secured	**Unsecured**	**Total**	**Secured**	**Unsecured**	**Total**
Debenture loans	8	7,526	7,534	18	6,867	6,885
Capital lease obligations	1,240	—	1,240	1,546	—	1,546
Banks and other:						
• Fixed rate	179	1,025	1,204	294	1,053	1,347
• Floating rate	754	9,515	10,269	62	7,480	7,542
	933	10,540	11,473	356	8,533	8,889
TOTAL	**2,181**	**18,066**	**20,247**	**1,920**	**15,400**	**17,320**

Debenture loans can be analyzed as follows:

December 31,	1992	1991
PARENT COMPANY		
7½%-9% Convertible Bonds 1979-92 (*)	—	28
11.55% Single Coupon Bonds 1985-97 and accrued interest	1,165	1,044
5⅞% Bonds 1984-94 (Swiss franc 80 million)	157	160
3⅛% Notes 1988-95 (Swiss franc 100 million)	375	352
7⅝% Bonds 1988-93 (Ecu 50 million)	307	288
8⅝% Bonds 1989-93 (French franc 500 million)	416	391
9% Bonds 1989-94 (Ecu 50 million)	303	285
9½% Bonds 1991-98 (French franc 750 million)	721	678
10½% Bonds 1991-96 (Canadian dollar 100 million)	481	454
9¼% Notes 1991-96 (Luxemburg franc 600 million)	94	88
8½% Bonds 1991-2001 (German mark 200 million)	700	658
7⅛% Bonds 1991-2001 (Swiss franc 100 million)	398	375
8¼% Bonds 1992-2002 (German mark 300 million)	996	—
Short-term portion (**)	(738)	(43)
Total Parent Company	**5,375**	**4,758**
TRD		
9½% GOBTP Bonds 1973-93 (French franc 20 million)	3	6
TMO Bonds 1982-92 (French franc 750 million)	—	750
11¼% Bonds 1984-94 (French franc 500 million)	500	500
11.55% Single Coupon Bonds 1985-97 and accrued interest	1,151	964
TMO Bonds 1985-95 (French franc 500 million)	500	500
Short-term portion (**)	(3)	(753)
Total TRD	**2,151**	**1,967**
Other consolidated subsidiaries	8	160
TOTAL	**7,534**	**6,885**

(*) Including amortization premium.
(**) Bonds due within one year:
- as of December 31, 1992:
  - 7⅝% Bonds 1988-93 (French franc 307 million),
  - 8⅝% Bonds 1989-93 (French franc 416 million),
  - 5⅞% Bonds 1984-94 (French franc 15 million),
  - 9½% GOBTP Bonds 1973-93 (French franc 3 million).
- as of December 31, 1991:
  - 7½%-9% Convertible Bonds 1979-92 (French franc 28 million),
  - 5⅞% Bonds 1984-94 (French franc 15 million),
  - TMO Bonds 1982-92 (French franc 750 million),
  - 9½% GOBTP Bonds 1973-93 (French franc 3 million).

Loan repayment schedule:

December 31,	1992	%	1991	%
1993	—	—	2,410	14
1994	3,439	17	3,599	21
1995	2,880	14	1,731	10
1996	2,470	12	1,482	8
1997 and after	4,785	24	8,098	47
1998 and after	6,673	33	—	—
TOTAL	**20,247**	**100**	**17,320**	**100**

Analyses by currency and interest rates:

These analyses are presented after the impact of interest rate and currency swaps.

December 31,	1992	%	1991	%
French franc	5,070	25	5,213	30
US dollar	7,649	38	6,821	39
Pound sterling	4,676	23	3,941	23
Canadian dollar	57	—	253	2
Dutch guilder	627	3	509	3
Swiss franc	101	—	84	—
Norwegian krone	1,656	8	13	—
Other currencies	411	3	486	3
TOTAL	**20,247**	**100**	**17,320**	**100**

December 31,	1992	1991
Fixed rates:		
below 9.25%	2,516	958
9.25% to 11.30%	554	451
11.30% and over	1,712	1,331
Floating rates	15,465	14,580
TOTAL	**20,247**	**17,320**

As of December 31, 1992, the parent company had an amount of US$ 2,080 million of long-term lines of credit, of which US$ 1,840 million were not used (US$ 2,040 million and US$ 1,943 million, respectively, as of December 31, 1991).

These facilities are primarily with international banks and extend for periods up to 10 years (with an average maturity of approximately 2.4 years). Interest on borrowings under these agreements are based on prevailing money market rates and are subject to various commitment fees on the unused portions of the lines of credit.

19. OTHER CREDITORS AND ACCRUED LIABILITIES

December 31,	1992	1991
Advances from customers and commercial current accounts	1,812	1,610
Accruals and deferred income	321	305
Payables to states (including taxes)	5,624	6,984
Payroll	1,587	1,549
Other	1,991	1,896
TOTAL	**11,335**	**12,344**

20. BUSINESS SEGMENT INFORMATION

The Company's primary business is the exploration and production of crude oil and natural gas and the refining and marketing of petroleum products.

The upstream operations of the Company are conducted through two segments:

- Exploration and Production is responsible for the Company's exploration and production activities outside of the Middle East;
- Trading and Middle East is responsible for those activities in the Middle East. The Trading and Middle East segment also conducts the Company's trading and shipping activities worldwide.

The Company's downstream operations are conducted through the Refining and Marketing segment.

Other segments are Chemicals organized into five divisions (rubber processing, resins, inks, paints and adhesives) and Mining.

The Company's other activities, not falling within these five segments, are grouped under the classification "Corporate" which also includes the residual corporate administration costs.

Operating profit and identifiable assets for each segment have been determined after making consolidation and intersegment adjustments as appropriate.

Sales prices between business segments approximate market prices.

A summary of the Company's operations by business segment is presented below:

Year ended December 31, 1992	Exploration and Production	Trading and Middle East	Refining and Marketing	Chemicals	Mining	Corporate	Consolidation Adjustments	TOTAL
STATEMENT OF INCOME:								
• Sales to unaffiliated customers	6,787	39,159	70,345	18,744	1,133	440	—	136,608
• Intersegment sales	3,819	23,474	1,409	21	21	1,665	(30,409)	—
Total Sales	10,606	62,633	71,754	18,765	1,154	2,105	(30,409)	136,608
Operating income (loss)	2,939	488	2,150	1,660	79	(445)	—	6,871
Equity in net income (loss) of unconsolidated companies	(24)	45	(42)	4	—	16	—	(1)
Depreciation, depletion and amortization of tangible assets	1,804	89	1,799	761	111	110	—	4,674
Valuation allowances on tangible assets	—	—	4	—	—	—	—	4
Unproved properties depreciation (included in operating expenses)	50	—	—	—	—	—	—	50
Amortization and valuation allowances of intangible assets (Note 23)	(54)	11	95	70	—	14	—	136
Amortization of acquisition goodwill (Note 26)	8	—	217	319	27	14	—	585
Depreciation, depletion and amortization charged to income	1,808	100	2,115	1,150	138	138	—	5,449
OTHER INFORMATION								
Identifiable assets	24,445	8,104	42,711	18,719	1,473	20,148	—	115,600
Capital expenditures	6,664	519	6,059	1,822	209	144	—	15,417

Year ended December 31, 1991	Exploration and Production	Trading and Middle East	Refining and Marketing	Chemicals	Mining	Corporate	Consolidation Adjustments	TOTAL
STATEMENT OF INCOME:								
• Sales to unaffiliated customers	7,680	38,092	77,672	18,219	983	373	—	143,019
• Intersegment sales	4,909	27,320	938	21	62	1,726	(34,976)	—
Total Sales	12,589	65,412	78,610	18,240	1,045	2,099	(34,976)	143,019
Operating income (loss)	2,939	925	4,868	1,488	112	(550)	—	9,782
Equity in net income (loss) of unconsolidated companies	(25)	—	23	6	—	67	—	71
Depreciation, depletion and amortization of tangible assets	2,352	110	1,676	683	58	109	—	4,988
Unproved properties depreciation (included in operating expenses)	79	—	—	—	3	—	—	82
Valuation allowances on tangible assets	—	—	1	4	—	—	—	5
Amortization and valuation allowances of intangible assets (Note 23)	37	—	125	334	—	23	—	519
Amortization of acquisition goodwill (Note 26)	3	—	182	207	27	12	—	431
Exceptional oil and gas properties write down (Note 24)	155	—	—	—	—	—	—	155
Depreciation, depletion and amortization charged to income	2,626	110	1,984	1,228	88	144	—	6,180
OTHER INFORMATION								
Identifiable assets	23,051	7,478	41,297	19,615	1,710	20,904	—	114,055
Capital expenditures	6,960	262	4,761	2,472	413	453	—	15,321

21. SALES BY GEOGRAPHIC AREAS

Sales of the Company are predominantly made in Europe and North and South America for refined products and in the Far East for crude-oil. The Company's sales by geographic areas are analyzed below:

Year ended December 31,	1992	1991
France	58,092	64,304
Rest of Europe	36,738	39,448
North and South America	19,855	21,605
Africa	9,413	10,217
Far East and rest of the world	42,919	42,421
Intersegment elimination	(30,409)	(34,976)
TOTAL	**136,608**	**143,019**

22. INTEREST INCOME (EXPENSE)

Year ended December 31,	1992	1991
Interest income	1,552	1,728
Dividend income	281	461
Interest expense	(2,863)	(2,983)
Less amounts capitalized	283	188
TOTAL	**(747)**	**(606)**

23. OTHER INCOME (EXPENSE)

Year ended December 31,	1992	1991
Foreign exchange gains (losses)	(331)	(439)
Gains (losses) on disposal of assets	355	270
Amortization and valuation allowances on intangible assets	(136)	(519)
Other	(43)	(121)
TOTAL	**(155)**	**(809)**

24. NON-RECURRING ITEMS

Year ended December 31,	1992	1991
(Allowances) Write-backs of provisions on:		
• Restructuring costs (a)	(276)	(300)
• Oil and gas properties write-down	—	(155)
• Termination plans and pension plans (b)	(230)	(133)
• Sector risks	270	209
• Extraordinary tax expenses	(141)	91
Refined petroleum products inventories at FIFO (TRD)	(162)	—
TOTAL	**(539)**	**(288)**

(a) In 1992, the Company has recorded an accrual on studies and development costs in the segment Trading-Middle East and restructuring costs on the Chemicals segment. Besides, some assets in the segment Refining and Marketing have been reduced to their realizable value.
The Company decided in 1991 to cease some of its operations in Chemicals segment and recorded in that scope an accrual for MFF 93. Besides, an exceptional write-down of the oil and gas properties has been recorded for MFF 207 in order to reduce the net assets in the United States of America to their realizable value.

(b) The termination plans accrued in 1992 are mainly to allocate to Refining-Marketing and Chemicals segments. In 1991, they were to allocate to the Refining-Marketing segment and the Parent company.

25. INCOME TAXES

In accordance with a consolidated tax agreement with the French Tax Authorities (Article 209 quinquies of the French Tax Code), the Company has been filing a worldwide consolidated tax return. The consolidated tax agreement provides that the basis for income tax computation is not limited to French or foreign consolidated subsidiaries or equity investees but also applies to direct or indirect shareholdings over 10% in the energy segment and over 50% in the other segments. It thus allows the Company to offset, within certain limits, the taxable income of profitable companies against losses of other entities.

On June 28, 1991, the Company obtained from the French Tax Authorities the renewal of this agreement for a five-year period which will end on December 31, 1995.

Besides, beginning on January 1, 1992, TOTAL exercised the option for its main French subsidiaries to apply the French group tax regime (Article 223A and followings of the French Tax Code).

Income tax expense:

	1992	1991
Current income taxes	1,458	1,644
Deferred income taxes	276	155
PROVISION FOR INCOME TAXES	1,734	1,799

Current income tax expenses represent the amounts paid or currently due to the local authorities for the period and is calculated in accordance with the rules and rates prevailing in the countries concerned after taking into consideration the tax agreements described above.

Deferred taxes are mainly provided on accelerated tax depreciation.

Deferred income taxes have not been provided on undistributed earnings of foreign consolidated subsidiaries to the extent such earnings are intended to be permanently invested in those subsidiaries.

Reconciliation between provision for income taxes and pre-tax income:

	1992	1991
Net income	2,847	5,810
Minority interest	216	32
Provision for income taxes	1,734	1,799
Less equity in income of unconsolidated companies	1	(71)
Pre-tax income	4,798	7,570
French statutory tax rate	34%	34%
French statutory rate applied to pre-tax income	1,631	2,574
Differences between French and foreign income tax rates	403	457
Permanent differences between accounting and taxable income	253	33
Effect of consolidated tax agreement, net	(75)	(839)
Unrecognized timing differences on French companies	(524)	(397)
Other, net	46	(29)
INCOME TAXES EXPENSE	1,734	1,799

26. AMORTIZATION OF ACQUISITION GOODWILL

Year ended December 31,	1992	1991
Goodwill amortized over 10 years	350	256
Goodwill amortized over 30 years	235	175
TOTAL	585	431

27. LEASES

The Company leases real estate, service stations and other equipment through noncancelable capital and operating leases.

The future minimum lease payments on noncancelable leases to which the Company is committed as of December 31, 1992 is set forth below:

	Operating leases	Capital leases obligations
1993	139	301
1994	96	264
1995	57	261
1996	43	191
1997	34	184
1998 and later years	62	764
FUTURE LEASE PAYMENTS	431	1,965
Less amount representing interest		(536)
Present value of net minimum lease payments		1,429
Less current portion of capital leases		(189)
LONG TERM OBLIGATION		1,240

Net rental expense incurred under operating leases for each of the years ended December 31, 1992 and 1991 was MFF 141 and MFF 16, respectively.

28. EARNINGS PER SHARE

Earnings per share are computed on the total number of common shares, of perpetual subordinated securities repayable in shares (TSDIRAs), of potential conversion in shares of employees share subscription plans, of convertible bonds and of warrants to purchase shares that were outstanding as of December, 31.

29. RELATED PARTIES

Year ended December 31,	1992	1991
RECEIVABLES		
Trade accounts	231	161
Loans and advances	1,892	1,417
PAYABLES		
Trade accounts	1,850	1,817
Loans and advances	104	—
Sales	962	788
Purchases	9,353	10,355

30. COMMITMENTS AND CONTINGENCIES

A summary of commitments given and received is as follows:

December 31,	1992	1991
COMMITMENTS GIVEN		
Discounted notes not yet matured	106	107
Guarantees given on customs duties	8,200	8,095
Bank guarantees	1,155	715
Other commitments given	2,651	1,423
TOTAL COMMITMENTS GIVEN	**12,112**	**10,340**
COMMITMENTS RECEIVED		
Guarantees received on customs duties	—	386
Commitments received on receivables	988	663
Other commitments received	1,570	572
TOTAL COMMITMENTS RECEIVED	**2,558**	**1,621**

Financial Instruments and Concentrations of Credit Risk The Company enters into financial instruments primarily to reduce its exposure to fluctuations in interest rates, foreign currency exchange rates and crude oil prices. The Company controls the credit risks associated with these financial instruments through credit approvals, investment limits and centralized monitoring procedures. In addition, the Company conducts its operations with customers located throughout the world which minimizes the risks on receivables. As a consequence, the Company does not anticipate non-performance by third parties which could have a significant impact on its financial position or results of operations.

Information on the financial instruments used by the Company:

December 31,	1992		1991	
	Commitments given	**Commitments received**	**Commitments given**	**Commitments received**
Long-term interest rate and foreign currency swaps	4,995	5,213	3,764	4,246
Long-term interest rate swaps	3,428	3,428	2,387	2,387
Short-term interest rate swaps	575	575	4,256	4,256
Short-term currency swaps	6,193	6,278	5,054	4,995
Caps/Floors contracts	—	600	—	1,059
FRA contracts	3,574	3,574	—	—
Interest rate futures	3,658	3,658	—	—
Currency option contracts	—	—	—	104
Options on futures contracts	417	417	—	31
Forward exchange contracts	365	375	—	—

Commodity contracts Off-balance sheet commitments related to the Company's operations on futures contracts of crude oil and refined products are as follows:

December 31,	1992		1991	
	Commitments given	**Commitments received**	**Commitments given**	**Commitments received**
In millions of US dollars	411	648	927	1,146

The contractual amounts stated above show the national commitment and are not indicative of gains or losses.

Legal Matters The Company is involved in various inquiries, administrative proceedings and litigation relating to contracts, sales of property, tax, antitrust and other matters. While any proceeding or litigation has an element of uncertainty, the Company believes that the outcome of any lawsuit or claim which is pending or threatened, or all of them combined, will not be significant to its consolidated financial position and results of operations.

Environmental The Company operates in an industry and in countries where regulations and laws concerning environmental protection are steadily increasing. Although it is impossible to predict accurately the effect of future developments in such laws and regulations, the Company does not expect that those contingencies will materially affect its consolidated financial statements.

31. EMPLOYEES SHARE SUBSCRIPTION AND SHARE PURCHASE PLANS

Share Subscription Plans The shareholders approved at the Extraordinary General Shareholders' Meeting held June 17, 1991 the implementation of share subscription plans under which the Board of Directors was authorized to grant to employees of the Company, during a five-year period, options to subscribe new TOTAL shares not exceeding 3% of the total number of outstanding common shares on the day when these options are granted.

In addition, the total number of unexercised outstanding options to subscribe granted under this share subscription plan and under the previous plan authorized by the Extraordinary General Shareholders' Meeting held June 20, 1986 may not exceed, at any time, 2% of the total number of the share capital.

The exercise period of options must be between six to eight years from the date of grant.

	Number of shares 1987 Plan (a)	Price per share	Number of shares 1988 Plan (a)	Price per share	Number of shares 1989 Plan (a)	Price per share	Number of shares 1992 Plan (b)	Price per share	Total number of shares
Options granted prior to January 1, 1991	197,000	F 97.5	387,000	F 77.5	216,000	F 77.5	—	F 225	800,000
Options exercised as of January 1, 1991	(97,096)		(208,228)		(121,120)		—		(426,444)
Options exercisable as of January 1, 1991	99,904		178,772		94,880		—		373,556
Options exercised	(75,604)		(72,480)		(19,800)		—		(167,884)
Options exercisable as of December 31, 1991	24,300		106,292		75,080		—		205,672
Options granted	—		—		—		788,700		788,700
Options cancelled	(7,400)		—		—		(2,000)		(9,400)
Options exercised	(16,900)		(76,692)		(16,800)		—		(110,392)
Options exercisable as of December 31, 1992	—		29,600		58,280		786,700		874,580
Expiration date	1992 March		1993 March		1994 March		1998 March 1998 June		

(a) Grants decided by the Board and authorized by the Extraordinary General Shareholders' Meeting held June 20, 1986.
(b) Grants decided by the Board and authorized by the Extraordinary General Shareholders' Meeting held June 17, 1991. The options are exercisable after a 3-year period from the date of grant.

Pursuant to the authorization of the Extraordinary General Shareholders' Meeting held June 17, 1991, the Board of Directors decided on December 17, 1992 to grant 700,000 options to subscribe shares. The individual grants must be made no later than October 31, 1993. As of December 31, 1992, no individual grant were made.

These options to subscribe shares will be exercisable under the following conditions:

- exercise price: FF 210,
- exercise period from the date of grant: 6 years.

The options are exercisable after a 3-year period from the date of grant.

Share Purchase Plans As approved by the Extraordinary General Shareholders' Meeting held June 12, 1989, the Board of Directors was authorized to make available to eligible employees options to purchase TOTAL shares. This program, limited to 1,200,000 shares, has been implemented as follows:

Board of Directors held January 24, 1990: 240,000 options granted at an exercise price of FF 112.5 per share.
Board of Directors held December 12,1990: 960,000 options granted at an exercise price of FF 148.5 per share. (a)

(a) 68,000 options have been cancelled in the context of this use.

The exercise period of the share purchase options is 5 years from the date of grant.

The number of unexercised options as of December 31, 1992 was 125,400 (Board of Directors of January 24, 1990) and 874,400 (Board of Directors of December 12, 1990).

The unexercised share purchase options were covered in full by shares held in treasury by the Company.

32. DIRECTORS AND OFFICERS COMPENSATION

Compensation paid to directors and executive officers of the Company amounted to MFF 26 and MFF 25 for the years ended December 31, 1992 and 1991, respectively.

33. PAYROLL AND STAFF

Year ended December 31,	1992	1991
PERSONNEL EXPENSE		
Wages and salaries (including social charges) (MFF)	11,658	11,346
AVERAGE PERSONNEL NUMBERS		
France		
• Executives	4,813	4,636
• Other	17,775	18,041
International		
• Executives	4,107	3,765
• Other	24,444	22,923
TOTAL	**51,139**	**49,365**

Average personnel numbers include employees of fully consolidated subsidiaries.

34. CONSOLIDATED STATEMENTS OF CASH-FLOWS

(I) Supplemental Schedule of Non-Cash Investing and Financing Activities

No significant non-cash investing or financing activities have been undertaken in 1992. In 1991, pursuant to the merger of OFP into the Company and the public exchange offer for Hutchinson, the shareholders' equity increased by MFF 1,484 and MFF 683, respectively. The conversion of TSDIRAs into new shares represented MFF 317 in 1992 and MFF 2,504 in 1991.

(II) Disclosure of Accounting Policy

The consolidated statements of cash flows exclude the currency translation differences arising from translation of assets and liabilities denominated in foreign currency into French francs using exchange rates prevailing at the end of the period (except for cash and cash equivalents). Therefore, the consolidated statements of cash flows will not agree with the differences derived from the consolidated balance sheet amounts.

Cash and Cash Equivalents Cash equivalents are highly liquid investments that are readily convertible to cash and have original maturities of three months or less. Bank overdrafts variations are included in cash provided by financing activities.

Long-term Debt Changes in long-term debt have been presented net to reflect that significant changes mainly related to revolving agreements. The detailed analysis is as follows:

Year ended December 31,	1992	1991
Increase in long-term debt	10,444	10,958
Repayment of long-term debt	(4,853)	(7,029)
NET INCREASE (DECREASE) IN LONG-TERM DEBT	**5,591**	**3,929**

Exchange Rate In relation with the change in the method of translation of statements denominated in foreign currencies, the consolidated statements of cash flows have been translated into French francs at the average exchange rate of 1992.

In the year 1991, the consolidated statements of cash flows were translated in French francs at the exchange rate prevailing at the end of the period.

35. OTHER INFORMATION

The TOTAL Group, within the context of its listing on the Paris Stock Exchange files a reference document with the Commission des Opérations de Bourse ("COB"). This document may be provided by the Company or authorized depositary banks.

Besides, the TOTAL Group, within the context of its listing on the New York Stock Exchange ("NYSE"), files an annual report under the form 20F with the US Securities and Exchange Commission ("SEC").

APPENDIX II

Extract from the Annual Report of Daimler-Benz, 1992

Financial Statements

Consolidated Balance Sheet

ASSETS	Notes	December 31, 1992 In Millions of DM	December 31, 1991 In Millions of DM
Non-Current Assets			
Intangible Assets	(1)	611	774
Fixed Assets	(2)	19,254	16,574
Financial Assets	(3)	3,991	3,758
Leased Equipment	(4)	9,777	8,092
		33,633	29,198
Current Assets			
Inventories	(5)	23,138	20,732
Advance Payments Received	(6)	(5,549)	(5,827)
		17,589	14,905
Receivables from Leasing and Sales Financing	(7)	6,166	4,255
Other Receivables	(8)	14,771	12,370
Other Assets	(9)	3,503	5,528
Securities	(10)	6,089	5,725
Cash	(11)	2,968	2,010
		51,086	44,793
Prepaid Expenses and Deferred Taxes	(12)	1,465	1,723
		86,184	75,714

STOCKHOLDER'S EQUITY AND LIABILITIES			
Stockholders' Equity	(13)		
Capital Stock	(14)	2,330	2,330
Paid-In Capital	(14)	2,117	2,117
Retained Earnings	(15)	13,440	13,182
Minority Interests	(16)	1,228	1,214
Unappropriated Profit of Daimler-Benz AG		604	605
		19,719	19,448
Provisions			
Provisions for Old-Age Pensions and Similar Obligations	(17)	12,217	10,790
Other Provisions	(18)	22,478	17,239
		34,695	28,029
Liabilities			
Liabilities from Leasing and Sales Financing	(19)	10,971	8,113
Accounts Payable Trade	(20)	6,517	7,015
Other Liabilities	(21)	13,725	12,600
		31,213	27,728
Deferred Income		557	509
		86,184	75,714

Consolidated Balance Sheet

Consolidated Statement of Income

	Notes	1992 In Millions of DM	1991 In Millions of DM
Sales	(22)	**98,549**	**95,010**
Increase in Inventories and Other Capitalized In-House Output	(23)	2,330	3,556
Total Output		**100,879**	**98,566**
Other Operating Income	(24)	4,506	3,545
Cost of Materials	(25)	(49,084)	(49,456)
Personnel Expenses of which for Old-Age Pensions DM 1,539 million (1991: DM 1,511 million)	(26)	(32,003)	(29,372)
Amortization of Intangible Assets, Depreciation of Fixed Assets and of Leased Eqipment	(27)	(7,085)	(5,977)
Other Operating Expenses	(28)	(15,254)	(13,824)
Income from Affiliated, Associated and Related Companies	(29)	118	56
Interest Income	(30)	577	623
Write-Downs of Financial Assets and of Securities	(31)	(121)	(134)
Results from Ordinary Business Activities		**2,533**	**4,027**
Extraordinary Result	(32)	-	(544)
Income Taxes	(33)	(586)	(1,039)
Other Taxes	(33)	(496)	(502)
Net Income	(34)	**1,451**	**1,942**
Profit Carried Forward from Previous Year		2	8
Transfer to Retained Earnings		(816)	(1,275)
Income Applicable to Minority Shareholders		(184)	(99)
Loss Applicable to Minority Shareholders		151	29
Dividend (1991: Unappropriated Profit) of Daimler-Benz AG		**604**	**605**

Consolidated Statement of Non-Current Assets

In Millions of DM	Acquisition-/Manufacturing Costs				
	1/1/1992 *)	Additions *)	Reclassifi-cations	Deductions	12/31/1992
Intangible Assets					
Franchises, Industrial Property Rights and Similar Rights, as well as Licences to Such Rights	487	192	17	66	630
Goodwill	662	26	-	184	504
	1,149	**218**	**17**	**250**	**1,134**
Fixed Assets					
Land, Land Titles and Buildings Including Buildings Owned by Others	16,434	1,567	429	85	18,345
Technical Equipment and Machinery	21,258	2,480	796	777	23,757
Other Equipment, Factory and Office Equipment	16,275	1,840	610	1,173	17,552
Advance Payments Relating to Plant and Equipment and Construction in Progress	2,344	1,942	(1,852)	125	2,309
	56,311	**7,829**	**(17)**	**2,160**	**61,963**
Financial Assets					
Investments in Affiliated Companies	869	75	9	486	467
Loans to Affiliated Companies	11	2	-	2	11
Investments in Associated Companies	311	30	1,103	89	1,355
Investments in Related Companies	2,112	313	(1,079)	71	1,275
Loans to Related Companies	133	30	(37)	3	123
Investments in Long-Term Securities	551	14	-	48	517
Other Long-Term Receivables	875	183	4	109	953
	4,862	**647**	**-**	**808**	**4,701**
	62,322	**8,694**	**-**	**3,218**	**67,798**
Leased Equipment	**11,853**	**5,206**	**-**	**2,741**	**14,318**

*) Including carry-forward amounts of companies consolidated for the first time.

Amortization/Depreciation/Write-Downs					Net Book Value	
1/1/1992 *)	Current Year	Reclassifi-cations	Deductions	12/31/1992	12/31/1992	12/31/1991
306	135	-	54	387	243	181
69	73	-	6	136	368	593
375	**208**	**-**	**60**	**523**	**611**	**774**
8,167	859	-	84	8,942	9,403	8,267
17,933	1,966	17	679	19,237	4,520	3,325
13,607	1,844	16	959	14,508	3,044	2,668
30	30	(33)	5	22	2,287	2,314
39,737	**4,699**	**-**	**1,727**	**42,709**	**19,254**	**16,574**
559	2	-	448	113	354	310
2	-	-	-	2	9	9
45	46	-	5	86	1,269	266
302	2	-	-	304	971	1,810
4	1	-	1	4	119	129
22	2	-	3	21	496	529
170	30	-	20	180	773	705
1,104	**83**	**-**	**477**	**710**	**3,991**	**3,758**
41,216	**4,990**	**-**	**2,264**	**43,942**	**23,856**	**21,106**
3,761	**2,178**	**-**	**1,398**	**4,541**	**9,777**	**8,092**
					33,633	**29,198**

Notes to the Consolidated Financial Statements

Principles and Methods

The consolidated financial statements have been prepared in accordance with regulations set forth in the Commercial Code; the amounts are shown in millions of D-marks. The items, which are summarized in the balance sheet and the statement of income, are separately shown in the notes and, where necessary, explained.

Deviating from the previous year, we additionally show in the consolidated financial statements – apart from the caption "leased vehicles and equipment" – the captions "receivables from sales financing" and "liabilities from leasing and sales financing", in order to accomodate the pecularities of the financial services business.

Accounting Principles and Valuation Methods

During the year under review, we have continued to apply the same accounting principles and valuation methods. Assets and liabilities presented in the consolidated balance sheet – in identical group circumstances – are uniformly valued. In 1992, as in previous years, provisions for approved conversion, reconstruction and maintenance projects have been set up, or have been systematically updated.

Intangible assets are valued at acquisition costs and are written off over the respective useful lives. Goodwill resulting from the capital consolidation, if derived from the extension of the group, is in principle amortized over five years; goodwill relating to the restructuring of the group is charged to retained earnings. Goodwill which arose from the creation of strategic alliances, is split. The portion relating to the group's expansion is written off over the relevant useful life, the one relating to the restructuring is charged to retained earnings.

Fixed assets are valued at acquisition or manufacturing costs. The self-constructed facilities comprise direct costs and applicable materials and manufacturing overheads, including depreciation allowances.

The acquisition/manufacturing costs for fixed assets are reduced by scheduled depreciation charges. The opportunities for special tax-deductible depreciation allowances were fully utilized, i.e. in connection with Section 7d of the Income Tax Act (environmental protection investment), Section 6 b of the Income Tax Act, Section 4 of the Regional Development Law and Subsection 35 of the Income Tax Guidelines.

Scheduled fixed asset depreciation allowances are calculated generally using the following useful lives: 17 to 50 years for buildings, 8 to 20 years for site improvements, 3 to 20 years for technical facilities and machinery, and 2 to 10 years for other facilities and factory and office equipment. Facilities used for multi-shift operations are depreciated using correspondingly lower useful lives. Buildings are depreciated using straight-line depreciation rates – and where allowable under the Tax Codes – declining rates. Movable property with a useful life of four years or more is depreciated using the declining-balance method. For movable property, we change from the declining-balance method to the straight-line method of calculating depreciation allowances when the equal distribution of the remaining net book value over the remaining useful life leads to higher depreciation amounts. Depreciation allowances on additions during the first and second half of the year are calculated using the full year or half-year rates, respectively. Low-value items are expensed in the year of acquisition.

Investments in *related companies*, and in *other long-term financial assets* are valued at the lower of cost or market; non-interest bearing or low-interest bearing receivables are shown at their present value. Major *investments in associated companies* are valued according to the book value method at equity.

Leased equipment is valued at acquisition or manufacturing costs, and is depreciated using the declining-balance method. We change from the declining-balance method to the straight-line method of calculating depreciation allowances when the equal distribution of the remaining net book value over the remaining useful life leads to higher depreciation amounts. The opportunities for tax-deductible depreciation allowances were fully utilized, i.e. in connection with Subsection 35 of the Income Tax Guidelines.

Raw materials and supplies as well as *goods purchased for resale* are valued at the lower of cost or market. *Finished goods* are valued at manufacturing costs which comprise, apart from direct material and direct labor, applicable material and manufacturing overheads including depreciation charges.

To the extent that inventory risks are determinable, i.e. for reduced usability after prolonged storage or after design changes, reasonable deductions are made, which are calculated based on a loss-free valuation.

Receivables and other assets – if non-interest bearing – are reduced to their present vaue at the balance sheet date, and are valued taking into account all known risks. A lump-sum allowance for doubtful accounts on a country-specific scale is deducted from the receivables in recognition of the general risk inherent in receivables.

Treasury stock is valued at the expected selling price to employees of the Daimler-Benz group. *Securities* are valued at the lower of cost or market value at the balance sheet date.

Provisions for old-age pensions and similar obligations are actuarially determined on the basis of an assumed interest rate of 6 % using the Entry Age Actuarial Cost Method. The regulations of the 1992 Pension Reform Act have been taken into account in calculating the provision amount.

Provisions for taxes and *other provisions* are determined on the basis of fair and reasonable business judgements. The obligations in the personnel and social area are reflected in the financial statements at non-discounted values expected to be paid in the future as benefits are vested.

Liabilities are shown at their repayment amounts.

Companies Included in Consolidation

The companies included in consolidation encompass, apart from Daimler-Benz AG, 271 (1991: 255) domestic and foreign subsidiaries and 7 joint venture companies.

During the year under review, 26 companies have, for the first time, been added to consolidation. Moreover, one joint venture company was included pro rata, for the first time, pursuant to Section 310 of the Commercial Code. A total of 10 subsidiaries and one joint venture company were deleted from consolidation.

Deutsche Aerospace Airbus GmbH and its subsidiaries were fully consolidated in the consolidated accounts effective January 1, 1992. Up to 1991, Deutsche Aerospace Airbus GmbH was only consolidated at equity in conformity with Section 296, Subsection 1, Paragraph 1 of the Commercial Code. After the transfer by the Kreditanstalt für Wiederaufbau of its 20 % stake in Deutsche Aerospace Airbus GmbH to DASA, this limitation with respect to excercising its rights no longer applies, which, on account of agreements with the Federal Republic of Germany and of rules in the bylaws, had existed up to that point.

The first-time consolidation of the Deutsche Aerospace Airbus group effected both the consolidated balance sheet and the consolidated statement of income. These effects are explained under the relevant balance sheet and statement of income captions.

In 1991, only the balance sheet items of the Eurocopter companies were proportionally included in consolidation because of their relatively short affiliation with the group; in 1992, they were included in the statement of income as well.

Because income and expense items relative to the German helicopter activities were still included in the 1991 accounts, comparability of group financial statements with the previous year is not materially affected.

Not included are 248 subsidiaries, whose effect on the assets, liabilities, financial position and results of operations of the group is not material (their total sales volume is less than 1 % of consolidated sales), and 11 companies administering pension funds whose assets are subject to restrictions.

Principles of Consolidation

Capital consolidation was effected according to the book value method where the parent's acquisition costs are eliminated against the relevant share capital and retained earnings at the time of acquisition or first-time inclusion in consolidation. This applies analogously to the joint venture companies that were included pro rata.

The differences resulting from the capital consolidation (debit balance) are, as far as possible, allocated to the relevant balance sheet items and are written off to income over their useful lives. For the treatment of the remaining differences (goodwill), see explanations under "accounting principles and valuation methods". The remaining goodwill resulting from the addition of the *joint venture companies* of the Eurocopter group is shown under "intangible assets"; the portion applicable to the group's expansion will be amortized over a useful life of 10 years. The other portion was charged to retained earnings in 1992, without affecting income.

A difference (credit balance) resulting from the capital consolidation is shown under the balance sheet caption "other provisions" earmarked as "difference from capital consolidation with reserve characteristics".

Profits earned by subsidiaries after the date of acquisition are added to consolidated retained earnings. The unappropriated profit shown in the financial statements corresponds to the dividend payout proposed by Daimler-Benz AG. For this reason we have charged the income-affecting consolidation adjustments and the profits earned by our subsidiaries to consolidated retained earnings.

The consolidated financial statements include 127 *associated companies.*

At year-end, 13 associated companies have been included in our consolidated financial statements according to the *book value method* at equity.

The remaining associated companies are shown under investments in affiliated companies at acquisition costs – in some instances less write-downs – as they are not material to the consolidated assets, liabilities, financial position and results of operations.

The 34 % stake in Sogeti S. A., Grenoble, which was acquired by Daimler-Benz AG in December of 1991, was transferred to debis AG in October 1992. As of December 31, 1992, Sogeti was included in consolidation at equity according to the book value method. However, only the 1991 accounts were used because Sogeti's 1992 financials had not been available at the time the Daimler-Benz consolidated financial statements were prepared. The goodwill of DM 355 million will be amortized over 15 years.

Intercompany receivables and payables have been eliminated; the differences resulting from *debt consolidation* have been charged or credited to income.

All material *intercompany profits* resulting from the intercompany sales of goods and services have been eliminated, except items of minor importance. This also applies to sales of goods and services by associated companies to companies included in consolidation.

Intercompany sales and other intercompany earnings have been eliminated against the relevant costs, or reclassified to "capitalized in-house output" or to "increase in inventories", respectively.

Deferred taxes (debit balance) shown in the consolidated balance sheet result from income-affecting consolidation adjustments.

Curreny Translation

Foreign currency receivables are translated in the individual financial statements at the bid price on the day they are recorded or at the spot rate on the balance sheet date if lower. Foreign currency payables are translated at the asked price on the day they are recorded or at the spot rate on the balance sheet date if higher.

The accounts of all foreign companies are translated to D-marks on the basis of historical exchange rates for non-current assets, and at year-end exchange rates for current assets, borrowed capital, and unappropriated profit. Stockholders' equity in D-marks is the remaining difference between translated assets less translated liabilities and unappropriated profit. The difference resulting from the translation of balance sheet items is recorded in consolidated retained earnings.

Expense and income items are essentially translated at average annual exchange rates. To the extent that they relate to fixed assets (fixed asset depreciation, profit or loss from disposal of fixed assets), they are translated at historical costs. Net income, additions to retained earnings, and the unappropriated profit are translated at year-end rates. The difference resulting from the translation of annual net income, between annual average rates and the exchange rates at the balance sheet date, is reflected in other operating income (1991: other operating expenses).

The adjustments made in the income statements by our subsidiaries in Brazil for monetary devaluations have been retained in the consolidated statement of income without change, effectively preventing reflection of inflationary profits. The income taxes, which were already geared to the balance sheet date in the national financial statements, have been translated at year-end rates.

Items from inflation-adjusted income statements of our Argentinian companies are translated at year-end exchange rates. Fictitious profits/losses resulting from the divergence between the inflationary trend and the changes in the currency's value have been eliminated.

Notes to the Consolidated Balance Sheet

1 Intangible Assets

Intangible assets, amounting to DM 611 million (1991: DM 774 million) comprise goodwill arising from the capital consolidation and from individual company financial statements, acquired EDP software, patents and, to a lesser extent, advance payments made. The decrease against the previous year is largely due to amortizations of goodwill charged to income and to the write-off of Eurocopter's goodwill to retained earnings.

2 Fixed Assets

The increase in property, plant and equipment by DM 2,680 million to DM 19,254 million is derived from additions of DM 7,829 million, of which DM 1,410 million represent net book values that are to be included within the scope of the first-time full consolidation of the Deutsche Aerospace Airbus group. These additions are reduced by re-classifications of DM 17 million, disposals of DM 433 million, and depreciation allowances of DM 4,699 million. Special tax-deductible depreciation allowances amount to DM 163 million (1991: DM 77 million); depreciation allowances in excess of scheduled depreciation amount to DM 21 million (1991: DM 39 million).

3 Financial Assets

A complete listing of our stock ownership will be filed with the commercial registry office at the county court house in Stuttgart under the number HRB 15,350.

Unscheduled write-downs, largely of investments in associated companies and of other long-term receivables totaling DM 83 million (1991: DM 115 million) had to be made.

Investments in non-current assets should have been written up by DM 7 million in accordance with the value appreciation doctrine (reinstatement of original values, Section 280 of the Commercial Code). However, such a write-up was omitted for tax reasons.

4 Leased Equipment

The increase in leased equipment – almost exclusively vehicles – by DM 1,685 million to DM 9,777 million, pertains largely to Mercedes-Benz Credit Corporation, Norwalk, U.S.A., and to Mercedes-Benz Leasing GmbH, Stuttgart. About 85 % of the balance sheet total pertains to these two companies. Special tax-deductible depreciation allowances amount to DM 3 million (1991: DM 10 million).

5 Inventories

in millions of DM	12/31/1992	12/31/1991
Raw materials and manufacturing supplies	3,342	3,041
Work in progress	8,836	8,160
Finished goods, parts and goods purchased for resale	9,694	8,557
Advance payments to suppliers	1,266	974
	23,138	20,732

Mercedes-Benz and Deutsche Aerospace account for the majority of consolidated inventories. The increase over last year is, with roughly DM 1,150 million, derived from the Mercedes-Benz corporate division, particularly from Mercedes-Benz AG and its foreign sales companies and with about DM 1,250 million from the DASA corporate division and DM 1,650 million as a result of the first-time, full consolidation of the Deutsche Aerospace Airbus group.

6 Advance Payments Received

Advance payments received amounting to DM 5,549 million (1991: DM 5,827 million) were almost exclusively for projects and long-term contracts at AEG, DASA AG, Dornier, Eurocopter and MTU; they were deducted from inventories.

7 Receivables from Sales Financing

This caption pertains to accounts receivable from customers totaling DM 6,166 million (1991: DM 4,255 million), of which DM 2,804 million (1991: DM 2,699 million) mature after more than one year.

8 Receivables
9 Other Assets

In millions of DM	12/31/1992	12/31/1991
Receivables from sales of goods and services	11,916	10,625
of which maturing after more than one year DM 491 (1991: 225) million		
Receivables from affiliated companies	1,178	335
of which maturing after more than one year DM 59 (1991: 11) million		
Receivables from related companies	1,677	1,410
of which maturing after more than one year DM 58 (1991: 596) million		
Total receivables	14,771	12,370
of which maturing after more than one year DM 608 (1991: 832) million		
Other assets	3,503	5,528
of which maturing after more than one year DM 394 (1991: 1,377) million		

Approx. DM 0.4 billion (1991: DM 0.3 billion) of the receivables from related companies pertain mainly to fixed-interest debt instruments and securities.

Other assets include investments of liquid funds in debt instruments not traded on stock exchanges. They amount to DM 437 million (1991: DM 2,564 million).

10 Securities

In millions of DM	12/31/1992	12/31/1991
Treasury stock	33	16
Other securities	6,056	5,709
	6,089	5,725

During the year under review, we purchased 225,511 common shares (par value DM 11.3 million = 0.48 % of the total outstanding share capital) at an average price of DM 709 a share.

In November of 1992, we sold 145,990 shares to our employees (par value DM 7.3 million = 0.31 % of the total outstanding share capital) at a preferential price of DM 469 for each share (in the event that one share was purchased) or DM 520 for each share (in the event that two shares were purchased).

We owned 122,287 common shares on the balance sheet date (par value DM 6.1 million = 0.26 % of the total outstanding share capital).

Other securities pertain mainly to fixed interest securities.

Within "current assets" there would have been a revaluation of DM 26 million necessary under the revaluation obligation. This did not take place due to tax law.

11 Cash

Cash amounting to DM 2,968 million (1991: DM 2,010 million) consists of deposits in financial institutions, cash on hand, deposits at the Bundesbank (German Federal Bank), in post office accounts, and checks on hand.

Liquid funds, shown among various balance sheet captions, total DM 9.8 billion (1991: DM 10.6 billion).

12 Prepaid Expenses and Deferred Taxes

Deferred taxes on income-affecting elimination entries amount to DM 1,329 million (1991: DM 1,596 million). Deferred taxes – a debit balance overall – as shown in the consolidated individual balance sheets are not included.

13 Stockholders' Equity

The changes in stockholders' equity are as follows:

	In millions of DM
Balance at 12/31/1991	19,448
Dividends paid by Daimler-Benz AG for 1991	(603)
Amount transferred from 1992 net income to retained earnings	816
Write-off of goodwill	(173)
Unappropriated profit of Daimler-Benz AG 1992	604
Change in stock ownership of minority shareholders	14
Difference from currency translation	(180)
Other changes	(207)
Balance at 12/31/1992	19,719

14 Capital Stock and Paid-in Capital

Capital stock and paid-in capital pertain to Daimler-Benz AG.

15 Retained-Earnings

Retained earnings comprise retained earnings allocated under statute of DM 160 million, retained earnings allocated for treasury stock of DM 33 million, and other retained earnings of Daimler-Benz AG of DM 8,534 million. Also reflected here are the company's share in the retained earnings and results of operations of consolidated subsidiaries, insofar as they have been earned by them since their affiliation with the group. Additionally, this caption takes into account the cumulative results from the elimination of intercompany earnings and from debt consolidation, as well as the difference arising from currency translations.

16 Minority Interests

The stock ownership of outside third parties in the subsidiaries included in consolidation pertain mostly to Daimler-Benz Luft- und Raumfahrt Holding AG, AEG, Mercedes-Benz of South Africa, Dornier, MTU and Eurocopter.

17 Provisions for Old-Age Pensions and Similar Obligations

Pension provisions rose to DM 12,217 million (1991: DM 10,790 million). DM 499 million of the DM 1,427 increase pertains to the change in the circle of consolidated companies.

When the assets of the provident funds are added to the provisions for old-age pensions, the company's pension obligations are fully covered.

18 Other Provisions

In millions of DM	12/31/1992	12/31/1991
Provisions for taxes	1,655	1,248
Difference from capital consolidation with reserve characteristics	21	44
Other provisions	20,802	15,947
	22,478	17,239

The provisions for taxes include DM 764 million (1991: 645 million) which pertain, to a large extent, to Daimler-Benz AG for open years awaiting final assessment.

The difference amount with reserve characteristics resulting from the capital consolidation originates from the first-time consolidation of one subsidiary; this amount will be available to offset potential extraordinary expenses during the start-up years.

Apart from existing warranty obligations, other provisions take into account, above all, obligations in the personnel and social area, risks for losses inherent in pending business transactions, and risks arising from contractual liabilities and pending litigation.

Additional provisions exist for expenditures which are based on approved change-over, alteration and some development projects, for possible additional costs in connection with completed contracts, and for maintenance which had been planned for the year under review but had to be deferred until the following year. In addition, provisions have been recorded for future obligations in connection with restructuring activities.

The DM 5,239 million increase pertains with DM 4,028 to the Deutsche Aerospace Airbus Group which was consolidated via DASA.

19 Liabilities From Leasing and Sales Financing

In millions of DM		12/31/1992	12/31/1991
Bonds		3,864	3,888
of which due within one year	DM 323 (1991: 379) million		
more than 5 years	DM 1,664 (1991: 1,407) million		
Debentures		3,471	1,468
of which due within one year	DM 3,471 (1991: 1,468) million		
Liabilities to financial institutions		3,024	2,417
of which due within one year	DM 1,808 (1991: 1,171) million		
Notes payable		140	108
of which due within one year	DM 140 (1991: 108) million		
Liabilities to related companies		132	70
of which due within one year	DM 101 (1991: 70) million		
Miscellaneous liabilities		340	162
of which due within one year	DM 86 (1991: 152) million		
Total liabilities from leasing and sales financing		10,971	8,113
of which due within one year	DM 5,929 (1991: 3,348) million		
more than 5 years	DM 1,664 (1991: 1,407) million		

The liabilities from leasing and sales financing serve the refinancing of leased vehicles and equipment and of receivables derived from sales financing. The caption debentures comprises commercial paper denominated in U.S. dollars; they are shown at the issue price plus accrued interest.

Miscellaneous liabilities comprise loans payable, and interest accruals in connection with sales financing.

The liabilities due to leasing and Sales financing are secured by pledging redeemable bonds in the order of DM 45 million (1991: DM 77 million).

20 Accounts Payable Trade
21 Other Liabilities

In millions of DM		12/31/1992	12/31/1991
Accounts payable trade		6,517	7,015
of which due within one year	DM 6,496 (1991: 6,890) million		
Financial liabilities			
Bonds		1,436	1,115
of which due within one year	DM 409 (1991: 255) million		
in more than five years	DM 417 (1991: 127) million		
Debentures		202	406
of which due within one year	DM 202 (1991: 406) million		
Liabilities to financial institutions		4,300	2,963
of which due within one year	DM 3,227 (1991: 1,916) million		
in more than five years	DM 227 (1991: 316) million		
Notes payable		174	433
of which due within one year	DM 89 (1991: 413) million		
in more than five years	DM – (1991: 7) million		
Other liabilities			
Liabilities to affiliated companies		1,090	1,613
of which due within one year	DM 941 (1991: 1,580) million		
Liabilities to related companies		1,782	1,349
of which due within one year	DM 1,384 (1991: 1,025) million		
in more than five years	DM 76 (1991: 86) million		
Miscellaneous liabilities		4,741	4,721
of which due within one year	DM 3,615 (1991: 4,030) million		
in more than five years	DM 355 (1991: 288) million		
of which for taxes	DM 906 (1991: 891) million		
of which for social benefits	DM 852 (1991: 823) million		
Other liabilities		13,725	12,600
Total liabilities		20,242	19,615
of which due within one year	DM 16,363 (1991: 16,515) million		
in more than five years	DM 1,125 (1991: 824) million		

Of the liabilities to related companies, about DM 130 million (1991: DM 370 million) pertain to liabilities to financial institutions. Excluding those, they pertain mainly to obligations by Deutsche Aerospace Airbus GmbH to Airbus Industrie G.I.E., Toulouse, as well as to liabilities at DASA relating to project companies.

Debentures pertain to commercial paper issued in D-marks; they are shown at the issue price plus accrued interest.

Miscellaneous liabilities largely comprise December 1992 accruals for wages and salaries as well as tax liabilities.

Liabilities to financial institutions, notes payable, liabilities to affiliated and related companies and miscellaneous liabilities are largely secured by mortgage conveyance, liens and assignment of receivables in the order of DM 1,091 million (1991: DM 1,231 million).

Contingent Liabilities

In millions of DM	12/31/1992	12/31/1991
Collateral	1,383	1,557
Discounted notes	221	218
Contractual guarantees	536	261
Pledges for indebtedness of others	9	7

In addition, we are liable for non-estimable compensatory payments, guaranteed by Deutsche Aerospace AG for 1993 and future years. For outside shareholders of AEG Aktiengesellschaft and of Daimler-Benz Luft- und Raumfahrt Holding AG, there exist claims for non-estimable compensatory payments.

Moreover, there exist contractual performance guarantees that could not reasonably be estimated.

Other Financial Obligations

Other financial obligations arising from rental, property lease and leasing contracts average approx. DM 748 million annually; the average contract duration is 8 years.

For companies not included in consolidation, we have other financial obligations amounting to DM 102 million; the average contract duration is 9 years.

In connection with the fiduciary settlement by Deutsche Aerospace Airbus GmbH of the federally guaranteed serial credits, the effective amount cannot be determined until the beginning of 1995 when the federal government's last tranche of DM 1 billion is due; this also applies to the reorganization profit received in 1989.

Within the scope of the government-supported Airbus-Development-Program, Deutsche Aerospace Airbus GmbH has agreed to assume performance portions itself. DM 331 million thereof relate to the time after the balance sheet date, to the extent that they are not already reflected in the annual accounts.

All assets acquired by Deutsche Aerospace Airbus GmbH with subsidy funds have been conveyed to the Federal Republic of Germany as security.

With reference to the development work for the Airbus program, Airbus Industrie G.I.E. has given a performance guarantee to Agence Executive (government office in charge of Airbus); this guarantee was taken over by Deutsche Aerospace Airbus GmbH – to the extent of its share interest – without restriction. Deutsche Aerospace Airbus GmbH considers the obligation arising therefrom fully covered by the relevant agreements for the financing and execution of the development work.

Beginning in 2002, the profit sharing agreement provides that the federal government will share in the profits of Deutsche Aerospace Airbus GmbH to the tune of 40 %. This rule, in its economic effect, stipulates the sequence of the government's repayment demands.

The remaining financial obligations, particularly purchase order commitments for capital investments, are within the scope of normal business activities.

The obligation arising from stock subscriptions and from capital subscriptions in close corporations pursuant to Section 24 of the GmbH Act, amount to DM 14 million.

We are jointly and severally liable for certain non-incorporated companies, partnerships and joint venture work groups. In addition, there exist performance contracts and miscellaneous guarantees in connection with ongoing business transactions.

Notes to the Consolidated Statement of Income

22 Sales

In millions of DM	1992	1991
Sales by corporate divisions: Mercedes-Benz	64,849	65,317
AEG	11,184	13,573
DASA	16,735	11,974
debis	5,781	4,146
	98,549	95,010

Sales for 1992 include for the first time DM 4.8 billion from the Deutsche Aerospace Airbus group.

	1992	1991
Sales by regions: Domestic	42,572	44,443
Foreign	55,977	50,567
Breakdown of foreign sales: EC countries	22,349	18,907
Other European countries	4,682	4,896
North America	13,881	12,969
Latin America	3,850	3,993
Other countries	11,215	9,802

23 Increase in Inventories and Other Capitalized In-House Output

In millions of DM	1992	1991
Increase in inventories of finished goods and of work in progress, including parts	944	2,111
Other capitalized in-house output	1,386	1,445
	2,330	3,556

24 Other Operating Income

The income amount included in this caption for the reversal of provisions totals DM 1,519 million. (1991: DM 893 million). Additional income is derived from exchange profits in connection with ongoing purchase and payment transactions, mostly earned abroad; exchange losses against such income are shown under other operating expenses. In addition, income is derived from costs charged to third parties, from security sales, and from rentals and leases.

Altogether, DM 2,226 million of other operating income is attributable to prior years.

25 Cost of Materials

In millions of DM	1992	1991
Cost of raw materials and supplies as well as of goods purchased for resale	43,951	44,340
Cost of services purchased	5,133	5,116
	49,084	49,456

In relation to a total output of DM 100,879 million (1991: DM 98,566 million), the ratio of cost of materials amounted to 49 % (1991: 50 %).

26 Personnel Expenses/ Employment

In millions of DM	1992	1991
Wages and salaries	26,138	23,813
Social levies and expenses for old-age pensions	5,865	5,559
	32,003	29,372

Employment (weighted annual average)	Number	Number
Wage earners	216,023	221,216
Salaried employees	150,650	144,101
Trainees/apprentices	15,960	16,194
	382,633	381,511

The 1992 employment figures for the first time include the employees of Deutsche Aerospace Airbus GmbH and its subsidiary.

In addition, 12,072 people are employed in the joint venture company Eurocopter.

27 Amortization of Intangible Assets, Depreciation of Fixed Assets and of Leased Equipment

In millions of DM	1992	1991
Amortization of intangible assets	208	137
Depreciation of fixed assets	4,699	4,076
Depreciation of leased equipment	2,178	1,764
	7,085	5,977

The depreciation of fixed assets pertains with more than 50 % to Mercedes-Benz AG. The increase in depreciation of leasing equipment results from the growth of the leasing business of our domestic and foreign finance companies.

28 Other Operating Expenses

This caption comprises additions to provisions, maintenance expenses, administrative and selling expenses including sales commisions, rental and lease expenses, foreign exchange losses incurred in the normal course of business, freight-out, packaging, and the expenses in connection with the currency revaluation at our Brazilian subsidiary companies.

Overall, DM 161 million is applicable to prior years.

29 Income from Affiliated, Associated and Related Companies

In millions of DM		1992	1991
Income received from affiliated, associated and related companies		157	34
of which from affiliated companies	DM 26 (1991: 13) million		
Income from profit and loss transfer agreements		19	15
Profit (loss) from companies included at equity		5	22
Loss from profit and loss transfer agreements		(63)	(15)
		118	56

30 Net Interest Income

In millions of DM		1992	1991
Income from other securities, and from long-term financial assets		158	125
Other interest and similar income		2,724	2,222
of which from affiliated companies	DM 10 (1991: 19) million		
Interest and similar expenses		(2,305)	(1,724)
of which to affiliated companies	DM 26 (1991: 18) million		
		577	623

The net interest expense balance from leasing and sales financing before the elimination of group internal interest income and expenses at the leasing and financing companies amounts to DM −421 million (1991: DM −446 million).

31 Write-Downs of Financial Assets and of Securities

In millions of DM	1992	1991
Write-downs of long-term financial assets	83	115
Write-downs of marketable securities	38	19
	121	134

32 Extraordinary Results

In millions of DM	1992	1991
Extraordinary income	–	490
Extraordinary expenses	–	(1,034)
	–	(544)

33 Taxes

In millions of DM	1992	1991
Income taxes	586	1,039
Other taxes	496	502
	1,082	1,541

The decline in tax expenses is largely due to a decline in income in the domestic circle of companies included in the interlocking relationship with respect to taxes.

34 Net Income

Consolidated net income of DM 1,451 million has predominantely been earned by the Mercedes-Benz corporate unit. Special tax depreciation of fixed assets and tax-allowable write-downs of current assets have reduced net income only slightly. Also, future charges in connection with such write-offs will not be material.

APPENDIX III

Glossary of Some Accounting Terms in English, Spanish, French and German

ENGLISH	SPANISH
A	
account	cuenta
accountancy, accounting	contabilidad
accountant	contable (also bookkeeper), experto
accounts (annual)	cuentas
annual general meeting	junta general
appropriation	apropriación
articles (of limited company)	articulos de asociación
assets	activo
associated company	participación
audit	revisión de cuentas
auditor	auditor, censor de cuentas
B	
balance (on an account)	saldo
balance sheet	balance de situación, balance
bank	banco
bearer (share)	acciones al portador
bill of exchange	lettre de cambio
board of directors	consejo de administración
bookkeeping	teneduría de libros
books of account	libros contables
borrowings	capital a préstamo
buildings	edificios
business	negocios

FRENCH	GERMAN
poste (bookkeeping), compte (eg bank)	Konto (bookkeeping), Kontokorrent (current account)
comptabilité	Buchführung, Rechnungslegung
comptable	Buchhalter
comptes annuels	Jahresanschluss
assemblée générale ordinaire	ordentliche Hauptversammlung
affectation	Gewinnverwendung
status	Gesellschaftsvertrag
éléments de l'actif	Vermögensgegenstanden, Aktiva (side of balance sheet)
participation	Beteiligung, Beteiligungsgesellschaft
révision	Prüfung
commissaire aux comptes	Prüfer, Wirtschaftsprüfer
solde	Saldo, Stand (fixed assets etc)
bilan	Bilanz
banque	Bank, Kreditinstitut
porteur (action au)	Inhaber (Aktie)
effet	Wechsel
conseil d'administration (managing), conseil de surveillance (supervisory), directoire (one-tier structure)	Vorstand (managing), Aufsichsrat (supervisory)
comptabilité, tenue des livres comptables	Buchhaltung
livres comptables	Buchführung
endettements (total), emprunt (loan payable)	Kreditaufnahmen
bâtiments, constructions, immeubles	Gebäude
affaires, enterprise	Geschäft

ENGLISH	**SPANISH**
C	
capital	capital
capital gain	plusvalía
capital loss	pérdida de capital
capitalise (expenses to assets)	capitalizar
cash at bank	caja
cash in hand, in cash	efectivo
cash flow	flujo de caja
chairman	presidente
chartered accountant	contandor habilitado
cheque	talón, cheque
Civil Code	Código Civil
Commercial Code	Código de Comercio
company	sociedad, compañía, firma
consolidated	consolidado
contingent	contingencia
contract	contrato, convenio
conversion	conversión
convertible	convertible
corporation tax	impuesto sobre renta de la sociedad
cost (purchase cost)	costes, gastos
cost accounting	contabilidad analítica, contabilidad de costes, contabilidad industrial
costs	costes, gastos
credit	haber (bookkeeping), crédit
creditor	acreedor
currency	divisas
current assets	activo circulante, corriente
current value	valor corriente
current liabilities	pasivo circulante, corriente

FRENCH	GERMAN
capital	Kapital
plus-value	Veräusserungsgewinn, Kapitalzuwachs
moins-value	Kapitalverzehr
porter à l'actif	aktivieren
banques	Guthaben bei Kreditinstituten
caisse	Kasse, Kassenbestand
cash flow, autofinancement	cash flow, Finanzfluss
président, PDG	Vorsitzender
expert comptable (equivalent)	Wirtschaftsprüfer, Steuerberater
chèque	Scheck
Code Civil	Bürgerliches Gesetzbuch
Code de Commerce	Handelsgesetzbuch
société; compagnie (more general word)	Gesellschaft
consolidé	konsolidiert
éventuel	eventuell
contrat, convention	Vertrag
conversion (convertible debentures, foreign currencies)	Währungsumrechnung
convertible	Konvertierbar
impôt sur les sociétés	Körperschaftssteuer
coût, prix de revient, prix d'achat (purchase cost)	Anschaffungs- oder Herstellungskosten
comptabilité analytique	Kostenrechnung
frais, charges	Kosten
passif (balance sheet), avoir (bookkeeping), crédit	Passiva (balance sheet), Haben (bookkeeping), Kredit (loan)
créancier, créditeur	Gläubiger, Verbindlichkeit (liability; as used in accounts)
devise	Währung
actif circulant	Umlaufvermögen
valeur actuelle	Buchwert
dettes à court terme	kurzfristige Verbindlichkeiten

ENGLISH	SPANISH
D	
debenture	obligaciones
debit	debe (bookkeeping), cargo (balance sheet)
debt	deuda
debtor	deudor
deductible	deducible
deferred charge, deferred credit	gasto aplazar
deferred tax provision	tasación diferida
depreciation	depreciación, amortización (provision)
director	consejero vocal
direct overheads	gastos generales directos
discount	descuento
disposal (fixed assets)	disposición
distribution (dividend)	reparto
dividend	dividendo activo
doubtful debts	deudores morosos, saldos dudosos
E	
employee	empleados, personal
exchange (foreign)	cambio
exchange rate	tipo de cambio
expenditure, expenses	gasto
exports	exportaciones
F	
factory	fábrica
figure	cifra
finished goods	productos terminados
fixed assets	activo fijo, inmovilizado

FRENCH	GERMAN
obligation	Schuldverschreibung, Anleihe
doit, débit (bookkeeping), actif (balance sheet)	Soll (bookkeeping), Aktiva (balance sheet)
créance (not *dette* = liability)	Verbindlichkeit
débiteur	Schuldner
déductible	abzugsfähig
charges à répartir	Rechnungsabgrenzungsposten
provision pour impôt différé	Rückstellung für latente Steuern
amortissements (provision), dotation aux comptes d'amortissements (charge)	Abschreibung
administrateur	Mitglied des Vorstands (des Aufsichtsrats)
frais généraux directement imputables	direkte Gemeinkosten
descompte (bills of exchange)	Disagio (on debentures etc), Skonto (on invoices)
sortie de l'actif, cession	Abgang (fixed assets), Veräusserung
répartition	Ausschüttung
dividende	Dividende
créances douteuses	zweifelhafte Forderungen
salarié exceptionnel	Mitarbeiter ausserordentlich
change	Tausch
taux de change	Kurs
charges, dépenses	Aufwendung, Aufwand
exportations	Ausfuhr, Export
usine	Fabrik
chiffre	Zahl, Betrag
produits finis	Fertigerzeugnisse
immobilisations	Sachanlagen

ENGLISH	**SPANISH**
fixtures and fittings	mobiliaro y enseres
furniture	mobili
G	
goods	bienes, mercancias, productos
goodwill	fondo de comercio
gross	bruto
group	grupo
guarantee	garantía
H	
hire	alquilar
hire purchase	compra a plazos
holding company	compañia tenedora
I	
income	ingreso, renta
income tax	impuesto sobre la renta
indirect costs	costes indirectos
insurance	seguro
intangibles	activo intangible
interest	interés
interim dividend	dividendo provisional
interim report	extracto financiero provisional
investments	immovilizado financiero (securities)
investments in subsidiary and associated companies	participación
invoice	factura
issued (capital)	capital emitido

FRENCH	**GERMAN**
agencements, aménagements, installations	Betriebs- und Geschäftsausstattung
mobilier, meubles	Einrichtungsgegenstände
marchandises	Waren
fonds de commerce, (on consolidation), survaleur	Firmenwert, Geschäftswert (on consolidation)
brut	brutto
groupe	Konzern
garantie (eg for goods sold), caution (eg for third party's debts)	Bürgschaft (for debts), Gewährleistung (for goods sold)
louer	Miete
location-vente	Kietkauf
société mère	Muttergesellschaft
revenu	Einkommen
impôt sur le bénéfice	Einkommensteuer
frais indirects, frais généraux	indirekte Kosten
assurance	Versicherung
immobilisations incorporelles	immaterielle Wirtschaftgüter
intérêts	Zins; Anteil (ie share in)
acompts sur dividendes	Vorabdividende
rapport intérimaire	Zwischenbericht
investissements (eg in fixed assets)	Investitionen (in fixed assets etc), Finanzanlagen (in balance sheet), Wertpapier (in other securities)
titres de participation	Beteiligung
facture	Rechnung
émis	gezeichnetes Kapital

ENGLISH	SPANISH
L	
land	terrenos
law	ley
lease, leasehold	alquilar, arrendamiento
liabilities	deudas (creditors), pasivo (balance sheet)
limited company	sociedad anónima (SA) (public), sociedad limitada (SL) (private)
limited partnership (with share certificates)	sociedad en commandita
liquidity	liquidez
loans	empréstitos, préstamos
loan capital	capital a préstamo
long term	a largo plazo
loss	pérdida
M	
machinery	maquinaria
manager	gerente
market value	valor mercado
merger	fusión
minorities	participación de la minoria
minutes	actas
money	moneda, dinero
mortgage	hipoteca
motor vehicles	vehiculos

FRENCH	**GERMAN**
terrains	Grundstück
loi	Gesetz
bail, crédit-bail (leasing agreement)	Erbbaurecht (land and buildings), Leasingvertrag (equipment)
dettes	Verbindlichkeit (creditors), Passiva (balance sheet)
société anonyme (public), société à responsabilité limitée (private)	Aktiengesellschaft (public), Gesellschaft mit beschränkter Haftung (private)
société en commandite (par actions)	Kommanditgesellschaft (auf Aktien)
liquidité	Liquidät
emprunt (payable), prêt (receivable)	Anleihe (payable), Ausleihung (receivable), Kredit
emprunt à long terme	Fremdkapital
à long terme	langfristig
perte	Verlust, Jahresfehlbetrag (for the year), Bilanzverlust (after reserve transfer)
machines, matériel	Maschinen
gérant (SARL); directeur (SA—ie not on board)	Direktor, Geschäftsführer (GmbH)
au cours du marché, au cours du jour	Markwert, Zeitwert
fusion	Verschmelzung
intérêts minoritaires	Ausgleichsposten für Anteile im Fremdbesitz, konzernfremde Gesellschafter
procès-verbal	Protokoll
argent	Geld
hypothèque	Hypothek, Grundpfandrecht
matériel de transport	Kraftfahrzeuge

ENGLISH	SPANISH
N	
net	neto
nominal	nominal
notes to the accounts	anexo al balance, comentarios al balance
O	
office	oficina
ordinary share	acciones ordinarias
overheads	gastos generales
P	
paid up, fully paid	desembolsado
par	nominal
partnership	sociedad en comandita, sociedad comanditaria
patent	patente
pay, payable, paid	paga, a pagar
pension	pensión
pension fund	fondo de pensión
p/e ratio	proporciòn precio-ingresos
personnel	personal
plant	instalaciòn
preference shares	acciones preferentes
premium	prima
prepayments	pagos andelantados
price	precio
prior period	ejercicio anterior
private company	compañia privada de responsibilidad limitada
profit	beneficio, ganancia, utilidades

FRENCH	GERMAN
net	netto
nominal	Nennbetrag
annexe	Ammerkungen, Erläuterungen
bureau	Büro
action	Stammaktie
frais, frais généraux	Gemeinkosten
entièrement libéré	bezahlt, voll eingezahlt
nominale	pari
société en nom collectif	offene Handelsgesellschaft (OHG)
brevet	Patent
payer, à payer, payé	zahlen, zahlbar, bezahlt
pension	Pension, Altersversorgung
caisse de retraite	Pensionskasse
rapport cours/bénéfice	Kurs/Gewinn Verhältnis
personnel, effectif	Belegschaft
matériel	Maschinen
actions préférentielles	Vorzugsaktien
prime	Agio, Aufgeld
compte de régularisation actif, avance (on order etc)	geleistete Anzahlungen (down payments), Rechnungsabgrenzungs-posten
prix	Kurs, Preis
exercise antérieur	Vorjahr
société à responsabilité limitée (SARL)	Gesellschaft mit beschränkter Haftung
bénéfice, profit	Gewinn, Jahresüberschuss (for the year), Bilanzgewinn (after reserve transfers)

ENGLISH	**SPANISH**
profitability	rentabilidad
profit and loss account	cuenta de pérdidas y ganancias
production	producción
provision	provisión
proxy	procuraciòn
public company	azienda pubblica
purchase	acquisto
Q	
quoted	cotizada en bolsa
R	
rate	tasa, tipo
raw materials	materias primas
receipt	recibo
redemption	reembolso
registered office	domicilio social, sede social
registered (share)	acción nominativa
remuneration	remuneración
rent out, let	alquilar
replacement, replacement value	reposición
report	informe
report and accounts	memoria anual
research and development	investigaciones y desarrollo
reserve	reservas
results	resultados
revaluation	revalorizaciòn
revenue	ingresos, rédito
royalty	derechos

FRENCH	GERMAN
rentabilité	Rentabilität
compte de résultat	Gewinn- und Verlustrechnung
production, fabrication	Herstellung, Produktion
provision	Rückstellung
formule de procuration	Stellvertreter, Vollmacht
société anonyme (SA)	Aktiengesellschaft
acheter (verb), achats de matières et marchandises (noun)	kaufen, einkaufen
admis à la côte officielle d'une bourse de valeurs	am einer Börse notiert
taux	Zinssatz (interest rate), Kurs (quotation, exchange rate)
matières premières	Rohstoffe
quittance (piece of paper), recette	Einnahme (income), Quittung (upon payment)
remboursement	Tilgung
siège social	Sitz
action nominative	Namensaktie
rémunération	Vergütung
donner en location	Vermieten
coût de remplacement	Wiederherstellungswert
rapport	Bericht
plaquette annuelle, rapport annuel	Geschäftsbericht
recherche et développement	Forschung und Entwicklung
réserve	Rücklage (declared), Reserve (secret)
résultats	Ergebnis
réévaluation	Zuschreibung
revenu, produits	Ertrag, Einkommen, Einkünfte
redevance	Lizenzgebühr

ENGLISH	SPANISH
S	
salary	sueldo
sale, sell	ventas
security	títulos — valores, valores mobiliarios
share	acción, participación
share capital	capital social
shareholder	accionista
share premium	prima de emisión
shop	tienda
short term	a corto plazo
solvency	solvencia
source and application of funds	origen y aplicación de fondos
stocks (inventories)	existencias, stock
stock exchange	bolsa de comercio
straight line (depreciation)	de línea recta
subsidiary	filial, subsidiaria
sundry	varios
T	
takeover	oferta de adquisición
tax	impuesto
tools	herramientas, utillaje
trade mark	marca
trade union	sindicato

FRENCH	GERMAN
salarie	Gehälter
vente, vendre	Umsatzerlöse, verkaufen
sûreté (on loan), valeur mobilière (shares)	Sicherheit (re loans), Wertpapier (shares, bonds etc)
action (SA), part (SARL, partnership)	Aktie (AG); Anteil (GmbH)
capital social	Grundkapital (AG), Stammkapital (GmbH)
actionnaire	Aktionär (AG), Gesellschafter (GmbH)
prime d'émission (paid for in cash), prime de fusion (on merger), prime d'apport (paid for in assets)	Agio, Kapitalzuzahlung
magasin	Laden
court terme	kurzfristig
solvabilité	Zahlungsfähigkeit
ressources et emplois des fonds, tableau de financement (statement)	Kapitalflussrechnung, Bewegungsbilanz (balance sheet differences)
stocks, valeurs d'exploitation	Vorräte
bourse	Börse
linéaire	linear
filiale	Tochtergesellschaft, anhängiges Unternehmen, Beteiligung
autres, divers	sonstige, verschiedene
offre publique d'achat (cash), offre publique d'éxchange (securities)	Erwerb durch Aktienübernahme
impôt, taxe	Steuer
outilage	Werkseuge
brevet	Warenzeichen
syndicat	Gewerkschaft

ENGLISH	SPANISH
translations (currency)	conversiòn
turnover	ventas
U	
unquoted	no cotizado
V	
valuation	valoración
value	valor
value added tax (VAT)	impuesto sobre el valor añadido (IVA)
variable	variables
variance	variaciòn
W	
wages	salarios
working capital	capital circulante
work in progress	productos en curso
Y	
yield	rendabilidad

FRENCH	GERMAN
conversion	Umrechnung
chiffre d'affaires, ventes	Umsatz
non admis á la côte officielle d'une bourse de valeurs	nicht notiert
évaluation	Bewertung
valeur	Wert
taxe sur la valeur ajoutée (TVA)	Mehrwertsteuer, Umsatzsteuer
variable	leistungstabhängig
écart	Abweichung
salaires	Löhne
fonds de roulement	Betriebsmittel
produits ou travaux en cours	unfertige Erzeugnisse
rendement	Rendite

Index